W9-DIJ-491

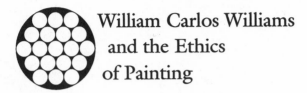

William Carlos Williams
and the Ethics
of Painting

William Carlos Williams and the Ethics of Painting

Terence Diggory

PRINCETON UNIVERSITY PRESS

PRINCETON, NEW JERSEY

Copyright © 1991 by Princeton University Press
Published by Princeton University Press,
41 William Street, Princeton, New Jersey 08540
In the United Kingdom: Princeton University Press, Oxford

Library of Congress Cataloging-in-Publication Data

Diggory, Terence, 1951–
William Carlos Williams and the ethics of
painting / Terence Diggory.
p.   cm.
Includes bibliographical references and index.
ISBN 0-691-06852-6 (cloth : acid-free paper)
1. Williams, William Carlos, 1883–1963—Knowledge—
Art   2. Williams, William Carlos, 1883–1963—Ethics.
3. Art and literature—United States—History—20th
century   4. Bruegel, Pieter, ca. 1525–1569—Influence.
5. Ethics in literature.   6. Ethics in art.   I. Title.
PS3545.I544Z5845   1991
811'.52—dc20   90-8995

This book has been composed in Postscript Galliard

Princeton University Press books are printed on acid-free paper,
and meet the guidelines for permanence and durability of the
Committee on Production Guidelines for Book Longevity of
the Council on Library Resources

Printed in the United States of America by
Princeton University Press, Princeton, New Jersey

10 9 8 7 6 5 4 3 2 1

For Anne

 *Contents*

⬡ List of Illustrations

1. Roy Lichtenstein, *Yellow and Red Brushstrokes* (1966). Canvas. 68 × 80 in. © Roy Lichtenstein. By permission: Leo Castelli Gallery/ VAGA.

2. Peter Brueghel the Elder, *The Peasant Dance* (ca. 1567). Panel. 70.5 × 97 cm. Kunsthistorisches Museum, Vienna.

3. Albrecht Dürer, *Draftsman Drawing a Nude*, from Dürer, *Unterweysung der Messung* (Nuremberg, 1538). Woodcut. 8 × 22.5 cm. The British Museum, London. Courtesy of the Trustees of the British Museum.

4. Jan Vermeer, *The Music Lesson* (ca. 1662). Canvas. 73.6 × 64.1 cm. The Royal Collection, London. Copyright reserved to Her Majesty Queen Elizabeth II.

5. Peter Brueghel the Elder, *The Adoration of the Kings* (1564). Panel. 108 × 83 cm. The National Gallery, London. By permission: The Trustees.

6. Aphrodite from Cyrene (2d cent. A.D. Roman copy from 4th cent. B.C. Greek original). Marble. H. 149 cm. Museo Nazionale Romano delle Terme, Rome.

7. Jean Fouquet (attrib.), *The Jester Gonella* (1st half 15th cent.). Panel. 36 × 24 cm. Kunsthistorisches Museum, Vienna.

8. Peter Brueghel the Elder, *The Massacre of the Innocents* (ca. 1565–1567). Panel. 111 × 160 cm. Kunsthistorisches Museum, Vienna.

9. Peter Brueghel the Elder, *Big Fish Eat Little Fish* (1557). Engraving. 22 × 29 cm. The British Museum, London. Courtesy of the Trustees of the British Museum.

10. Fra Angelico, *Annunciation* (ca. 1440). Fresco. 230 × 321 cm. Museo San Marco, Florence. By permission: Alinari/Art Resource.

11. Dying lioness (Assyrian, 7th cent. B.C.). Limestone. H. 13 3/4 in. The British Museum, London. Courtesy of the Trustees of the British Museum.

 *Acknowledgments*

THIS BOOK was completed during a leave of absence from Skidmore College generously arranged by Phyllis Roth, as Chair of the English Department, and Eric Weller, as Dean of the Faculty. A Skidmore College Faculty Research Grant helped to defray the expenses of securing permissions. Additional support was provided by a 1983 Summer Stipend and a 1984–1985 Fellowship for College Teachers awarded by the National Endowment for the Humanities, and by an appointment as Scholar-in-Residence in the Faculty Resources Network at New York University. The arrangements for that residency were coordinated by David Seligman at Skidmore and Leslie Berlowitz, Sidney Borowitz, and Ernest Gilman at New York University.

Correspondence with Richard Stamelman kept me alive to the broader theoretical implications and the international dimensions of the field in which Williams might properly be placed. Since Williams scholarship has itself become a field traversed by many paths, I might easily have lost my way without the expert guidance of Christopher MacGowan, who patiently answered numerous questions as my research evolved and carefully read the entire manuscript as it approached its final form. Suzanne Ferguson and Arthur Marotti kindly invited and then applied rigorous editorial standards to a preliminary formulation of my ideas that appeared in *Criticism*. At various stages I benefited from the comments of other readers: Christopher Collins, Harry Gaugh, Ernest Gilman, Barry and Lorrie Goldensohn, Steve Goodwin, Ann Hurley, Judith Kennedy, Stephen Melville, and Robert Miklitsch. Particular queries were kindly answered by James Laughlin, Paul Mariani, Carl Rapp, Stacy F. Roth, Leon S. Roudiez, Webster Schott, Linda Smith, Thomas Whitaker, and Patricia Willis. Giuseppe Faustini, Christina Giorcelli, Penny Jolly, Henry Sayre, and Joanna Zangrando offered invaluable advice and assistance in the collecting of illustrations, and Taylor Conard assisted in their preparation. As always, the Skidmore College librarians cheerfully responded to requests that at times must have seemed both trivial and burdensome.

Robert Brown of Princeton University Press offered support and encouragement at several crucial stages of this project. The interdisciplinary conversation that seems to arise spontaneously in the Skidmore College community, both inside and outside the classroom, supplied the essential climate for its germination. At home, Anne, Ariel, and Kelsey provided the ground from which it grew. To them, as to all those either named or implied above, I am deeply grateful.

• • •

Acknowledgment for rights to photoreproduction will be found in the list of illustrations. This is the place to acknowledge permission to quote from the work of William Carlos Williams as follows:

The Autobiography of William Carlos Williams. Copyright 1948, 1951 by William Carlos Williams. Reprinted by permission of New Directions Publishing Corporation.

The Build-Up. Copyright 1946, 1952 by William Carlos Williams. Reprinted by permission of New Directions Publishing Corporation.

Collected Poems: Volume 1, 1909–1939. Copyright 1938 by New Directions Publishing Corporation. Copyright © 1982, 1986 by William Eric Williams and Paul H. Williams. Reprinted by permission of New Directions Publishing Corporation and Carcanet Press Ltd.

Collected Poems: Volume 2, 1939–1963. Copyright 1944, 1953, Copyright © 1962 by William Carlos Williams. Copyright © 1988 by William Eric Williams and Paul H. Williams. Reprinted by permission of New Directions Publishing Corporation and Carcanet Press Ltd.

The Farmers' Daughters. Copyright 1934, 1950 by William Carlos Williams. Copyright © 1957 by Florence H. Williams. Reprinted by permission of New Directions Publishing Corporation.

I Wanted to Write a Poem. Copyright © 1958 by William Carlos Williams. Reprinted by permission of New Directions Publishing Corporation.

Imaginations. Copyright © 1970 by Florence H. Williams. Reprinted by permission of New Directions Publishing Corporation.

In the American Grain. Copyright 1925 by James Laughlin. Copyright 1933 by William Carlos Williams. Reprinted by permission of New Directions Publishing Corporation.

Interviews with William Carlos Williams. Copyright © 1936, 1939,

 *Abbreviations*

Alpers, Svetlana
AD *The Art of Describing: Dutch Art in the Seventeenth Century*. Chicago: University of Chicago Press, 1984.

BFP "Bruegel's Festive Peasants." *Simiolus* 6 (1972/73): 163–76.

SK "Seeing as Knowing: A Dutch Connection." *Humanities in Society* 1 (1978): 147–73.

Altieri, Charles
AQ *Act & Quality: A Theory of Literary Meaning and Humanistic Understanding*. Amherst: University of Massachusetts Press, 1981.

Dada "Abstraction as Act: Modernist Poetry in Relation to Painting." *Dada and Surrealism* 10/11 (1982): 106–34.

Freud, Sigmund
SE[vol.] *Standard Edition of the Complete Psychological Works of Sigmund Freud*. 24 vols. London: Hogarth, 1953–74.

Kristeva, Julia
DL *Desire in Language: A Semiotic Approach to Literature and Art*. Ed. Leon S. Roudiez. New York: Columbia University Press, 1980.

KR *The Kristeva Reader*. Ed. Toril Moi. New York: Columbia University Press, 1986.

PH *Powers of Horror: An Essay on Abjection*. Trans. Leon S. Roudiez. New York: Columbia University Press, 1982.

RPL *Revolution in Poetic Language*. Trans. Margaret Waller. New York: Columbia University Press, 1984.

TL *Tales of Love*. Trans. Leon S. Roudiez. New York: Columbia University Press, 1987.

Mariani, Paul

   NWN   *William Carlos Williams: A New World Naked.* New York: McGraw-Hill, 1982.

Mazzaro, Jerome

   LP   *William Carlos Williams: The Later Poems.* Ithaca, N.Y.: Cornell University Press, 1973.

Miller, J. Hillis

   Daedalus   "Williams' *Spring and All* and the Progress of Poetry." *Daedalus* 99 (1970): 405–34.

   ER   *The Ethics of Reading.* New York: Columbia University Press, 1987.

   LM   *The Linguistic Moment: From Wordsworth to Stevens.* Princeton, N.J.: Princeton University Press, 1985.

   PR   *Poets of Reality: Six Twentieth-Century Writers.* Cambridge: Harvard University Press, 1965.

   Views   *William Carlos Williams: A Collection of Critical Essays.* Ed. J. Hillis Miller. Twentieth-Century Views. Englewood Cliffs, N.J.: Prentice-Hall, 1966.

Riddel, Joseph N.

   Glyph   " 'Keep Your Pecker Up'—*Paterson Five* and the Question of Metapoetry." *Glyph* 8 (1981): 203–31.

   IB   *The Inverted Bell: Modernism and the Counterpoetics of William Carlos Williams.* Baton Rouge: Louisiana State University Press, 1974.

Sayre, Henry M.

   VT   *The Visual Text of William Carlos Williams.* Urbana: University of Illinois Press, 1983.

Williams, William Carlos

   A   *The Autobiography of William Carlos Williams.* New York: New Directions, 1967.

   BU   *The Build-Up.* New York: Random House, 1952.

   CP1   *The Collected Poems of William Carlos Williams* 1: 1909–1939. Ed. A. Walton Litz and Christopher MacGowan. New York: New Directions, 1986.

   CP2   *The Collected Poems of William Carlos Williams* 2: 1939–1962. Ed. Christopher MacGowan. New York: New Directions, 1988.

FD   *The Farmers' Daughters: The Collected Stories of William Carlos Williams.* New York: New Directions, 1961.

I   *Imaginations.* Ed. Webster Schott. New York: New Directions, 1971.

IAG   *In the American Grain.* New York: New Directions, 1956.

Int   *Interviews with William Carlos Williams: "Speaking Straight Ahead."* Ed. Linda Welshimer Wagner. New York: New Directions, 1976.

IWWP   *I Wanted to Write a Poem: The Autobiography of the Works of a Poet.* Ed. Edith Heal. New York: New Directions, 1978.

ML   *Many Loves and Other Plays: The Collected Plays of William Carlos Williams.* New York: New Directions, 1965.

P   *Paterson.* New York: New Directions, 1963.

RI   *A Recognizable Image: William Carlos Williams on Art and Artists.* Ed. Bram Dijkstra. New York: New Directions, 1978.

SE   *Selected Essays of William Carlos Williams.* New York: New Directions, 1969.

SL   *Selected Letters of William Carlos Williams.* Ed. John C. Thirlwall. New York: McDowell, Obolensky, 1957.

VP   *A Voyage to Pagany.* New York: New Directions, 1970.

Yale   Manuscripts in the American Literature Collection, Beinecke Rare Book and Manuscript Library, Yale University.

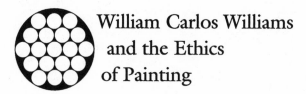

William Carlos Williams
and the Ethics
of Painting

# 1. The Heart of Describing

WILLIAM CARLOS WILLIAMS liked to tell a story about Alanson Hartpence, an acquaintance from the early years of Williams's career, when the new French painting had set the entire New York art world astir. In the Daniel Gallery, one of the first New York galleries to feature the new painting, Hartpence was on the verge of concluding an important sale. A collector had almost come to terms with one work Hartpence had showed her, but she called on him for a final clarification. As Williams tells it:

> "What is all this down here in this corner?" she said pointing to a part of the picture.
>
> Hartpence leaned over, inspected the area carefully, and after a little consideration stood back and said to the woman: "That, Madam, I should say, is paint."[1]

Similar anecdotes have been told on so many occasions that it now seems a matter of simple reflex to extract their moral: that the work of art is "about" nothing other than itself and must be judged solely on its own terms. The lesson that Williams draws, however, calls for reflection rather than reflex. He opens his lecture "An Approach to the Poem" (1947) with the Hartpence anecdote, in order to persuade his audience to view "the poem as an object, as a thing" (50), but by the end of his lecture, Williams makes clear that that thing is not his ultimate goal:

> *It is not merely to make a thing* called a poem on a piece of paper that the poet is working.
>
> It is to permit feeling to BE by making a vehicle for it. (63)

To permit feeling to be requires that Williams's aesthetic extend beyond the limits of formalism, ultimately into the realm of ethics. Because aesthetics and ethics remain closely intertwined, however, I have chosen to designate Williams's project "the ethics of painting."

Of all the arts, painting best represents Williams's project because of its combination of material and signifying properties. It is more palpably material than literature, and respect for material is a crucial tenet of Williams's aesthetic: paint is paint. On the other hand, compared, for example, with sculpture, the materials of painting are more obviously involved in a signifying process, like that which animates literature. As minimalism demonstrated, an art that seeks to produce mere "things" will move in the direction of sculpture, which has some chance of merely being the material that it is, perhaps because being and three-dimensionality are so intimately connected in our minds.[2] Painting, in contrast, tends to signify its materiality, a point made humorously in Roy Lichtenstein's nonpainterly translations of the abstract expressionist brushstroke (fig. 1). The formula "paint is paint" means also "paint refers to paint."

Williams's story about Alanson Hartpence suggests that his concern with these issues dates back to the second decade of this century, but it is significant that he began telling the story, at least in print, only in the late 1940s. In the years following World War II, the question of aesthetic autonomy, or self-referentiality, along with the still more fundamental issue of linguistic reference itself, was reposed in ethical terms that have continued to fuel critical debate since that time, although the terms themselves have occasionally gone unrecognized amid the heat they have generated. The new prominence assigned to ethics in the titles of recent critical works, which I have deliberately echoed in my allusion to an "ethics of painting," does not signal the emergence of a new concern but rather a new crisis in a concern of long standing.[3] Nor, as is sometimes charged, did that concern develop first abroad and then get imported to America, thereby precipitating crisis by its very foreignness. As the example of Williams would suggest, the roots of the crisis lie deep in native ground. They are as much the discovery of American writers as of French painters, and their implications have found explicit formulation in the critical trends that have arisen on both sides of the Atlantic since World War II. In this introductory chapter, it will be useful to survey those trends to provide a context for the more detailed examination of Williams that follows.

The art of abstract expressionism that arose in New York in the years immediately following World War II led the poet Frank O'Hara to reflect on the doctrine that "paint is paint," as Williams had done in response to earlier modernist art. Writing about Jackson Pollock in

1959, shortly after the painter's untimely death, O'Hara observed, "Very few things, it seems, were assimilated or absorbed by Pollock. They were left intact, and given back. Paint is paint, shells and wire are shells and wire, glass is glass, canvas is canvas."[4] This statement refrains from explicitly evaluating Pollock's procedure, but evaluation is implied in the enumeration of the physical materials of Pollock's art, which parallels a preceding list of qualities from the work of other artists that also supplied material for Pollock. In the latter instance, O'Hara approves of Pollock's procedure in ethical terms. Pollock, he writes, "did not appropriate . . . what was beautiful, frenzied, ugly or candid in others, but enriched it and flung it back to their work, as if it were a reinterpretation for the benefit of all, a clarification and apotheosis which do not destroy the thing seen, whether of nature or art, but preserve it in a pure regard."

Preservation is the positive value that O'Hara associates with Pollock, but it is not as if the materials that Pollock presents already exist for us in a pure state that the artist merely maintains against contamination. Rather, things exist for us only in our interpretation of them, but Pollock offers a reinterpretation that removes our earlier interpretations and permits us to see things as if for the first time, because we no longer see them as ours. As he admires Pollock's achievement, O'Hara appears to denigrate an activity for which Western artists, at least, have traditionally been commended: the appropriation of one's materials, taking possession of them, exercising mastery over them. Any transformation of the material can be viewed as evidence of such appropriation. O'Hara seems to have the surrealists in mind as a negative example when he says of Pollock, "You do not find, in his work, a typewriter becoming a stomach, a sponge becoming a brain." Such transformation, in O'Hara's view, is an act of violence that threatens to "destroy the thing seen."

Once this train of thought is set in motion, the violence that O'Hara opposes can be discovered in activities that appear much more normal than the surrealist metamorphosis to which he alludes. Inspired by investigations into the symbolism of dreams, surrealist imagery exposes the mechanism of any symbolic process in which one object displaces and comes to stand for another. This is the power of reference that I earlier attributed to painting. The ethical choices with which that power confronts the artist are essentially those that O'Hara outlines in his discussion of Pollock. Is paint to refer to paint, thereby preserving the material in a "pure regard," in O'Hara's phrase, or permitting feeling to be, in Williams's formulation? Or is paint to refer to something other than itself—an apple, a person, a Platonic form—and thereby serve that violence that channels the course of feeling or even represses it altogether?

The artist, Williams advised in "Against the Weather" (1939), "does not translate the sensuality of his materials into symbols but deals with them directly" (*SE* 197). The spreading of that conviction since World War II has led to an important critique of the symbolist aesthetic, understood not in the narrow sense of the French movement of the turn of the century but in the much broader sense of any art that refers beyond itself.[5] However, as that critique has been extended to the symbolic behavior informing all human activity, the prospects for an escape from the violence associated with symbolism have appeared increasingly bleak, at least to the eyes of the leading proponents of post-structuralism. Pronouncements such as Michel Foucault's, "we must conceive discourse as a violence that we do to things," or Jacques Derrida's, "writing cannot be thought outside of the horizon of intersubjective violence," read like despairing echoes of more hopeful statements by Williams and O'Hara.[6] Whether despairing or not, the post-structuralist attitude informs a methodology that has been applied to the reading of Williams. For instance, at the outset of his study of Williams's "counterpoetics," Joseph Riddel proclaims, "I have intended the violence, rhetorically and functionally, of my analysis" (*IB* xviii).

In opposition to such an intention, my main objective in this book is to examine the grounds for a critical practice that successfully resists violence, especially as Williams discovered those grounds in the art of painting.[7] Painting convinced Williams that there was an alternative to symbolism that was applicable also to Williams's own art of literature, and the manner in which Williams practiced his conviction was, at least at one time, capable of convincing others who shared his concerns. Perhaps the most important reader of Williams in this regard has been J. Hillis Miller, who explored an alternative to symbolism in his influential study *Poets of Reality* (1965), which reaches its climax in a chapter on Williams. In the introductory chapter Miller sets forth his premises in familiar terms: "An abstract expressionist painting does not 'mean' anything in the sense of referring beyond itself in any version of traditional symbolism. It is what it is, paint on canvas, just as Williams' wheelbarrow is what it is," that is, words on paper.[8] In his chapter on Williams, to convey a sense of how such poetry generates meaning, Miller again draws an analogy with painting: "Words as things incarnating their meanings become a set of fluid energies whose life exists only in the present. Such words, isolated and cleaned, can be put down on the page like splashes of paint on a canvas and allowed to explode into the multitude of meanings which emerge from their juxtaposition" (*PR* 304). This is a way of permitting feeling to be, as well as of "letting things be" (*PR* 306), since, freed of the bond of reference, words and things can exist independently of each other.

A strong undercurrent of ethical concern runs throughout Miller's argument. For instance, he compares the intellectual violence involved in the transformation of objects in symbolist art with the physical violence wrought by modern technology upon the natural environment (*PR* 4). However, in a move that is typical of much critical discussion since 1965, the structure of Miller's argument subordinates ethical questions to epistemological ones, making the former appear as means to the solution of the latter. By letting things be, fundamentally an ethical position, poets like Williams, according to Miller, were able to resolve the subject-object dualism that was inherent in Romantic or symbolist epistemology. "When man is willing to let things be then they appear in a space which is no longer that of an objective world opposed to the mind," Miller writes. "In this new space the mind is dispersed everywhere in things and forms one with them" (*PR* 8). Entrance into this new space earns Williams a place among Miller's "poets of reality," "reality" now being understood as lived experience, no longer as a separate world placed in opposition to consciousness.

The new sense of reality thus requires a corresponding renunciation of the privileged status of the agent of consciousness as a separate identity, an ego. Miller understands Williams to have undergone this renunciation at the outset of his career, in a "nameless religious experience" that Williams reported as such long after the event itself occurred, sometime around his twentieth year. Resigning himself to existence, or more precisely, resigning his sense of "private consciousness," as Miller interprets it, Williams received in compensation a sense of being "as much a part of things as trees and stones" (*SL* 147; cf. *PR* 287). At one with things, and thus relieved of the need to appropriate them for his special purposes, Williams is free to compose an art of "calm description," Miller's name for Williams's alternative to "the romantic or symbolist aesthetic of transformation" (*PR* 305).

Although its philosophical outlook ties *Poets of Reality* most closely to phenomenology, the importance Miller assigns to the simultaneous erasure of the external world and the ego points toward deconstruction, the new movement to which Miller quickly transferred his allegiance. In making that transfer, Miller left behind the analogy between painting and poetry, which, even in *Poets of Reality*, he had begun to question. Words cannot free themselves entirely of the power of reference, as abstract painting can, Miller assumes (*PR* 305). Later, in the light of deconstruction, Miller discovers that words, far from being a medium for conveying a poet's sense of his oneness with things, are already divided within themselves. Thus, in "Williams' *Spring and All* and the Progress of Poetry" (1970), an essay that enlists Williams in the cause of the "deconstruction of metaphysics" (*Daedalus* 419), Miller emphasizes the self-critical structure of *Spring and All* (1923), in which sections of prose and verse reflect on each other, though often only obliquely. "This structure of self-interpretation," Miller argues, "is characteristic in one way or another of all literature and of all art," by the very nature of linguistic reference (*Daedalus* 416). "Every poem has other poems anterior to it to which it refers in one way or another," Miller continues. "It also contains linguistic elements which are self-referential or 'metapoetical.' Some language in the poem is about the poem itself."

In just this way, I have argued, paint is about paint in modern abstract art. I take to be self-referential that practice that Miller, with regard to painting, assumes to be nonreferential, at least in *Poets of Reality*. Whether he retains that assumption in his essay on *Spring and All* is not clear; the "structure of self-interpretation" that he discusses there is said to characterize "all art," which would presumably include painting. But it is clear from the same discussion that, whatever arts it includes, the structure that Miller has in mind is defined by "linguistic elements." In the deconstructionist view that Miller is here in the process of adopting, language excludes any perceptual dimension. This exclusion entails a radical revision of the position of *Poets of Reality*, where, for instance, Miller argues that "reality comes to be present to the senses, present to the mind which possesses it through the senses, and present in the words of the poems which ratify this possession" (*PR* 11). In Miller's most recent essay on Williams, contained in the volume significantly entitled *The Linguistic Moment* (1985), Miller concludes that when Williams "at last takes possession of the presence of the present . . . it is a present . . . that is not perceptual but linguistic" (*LM* 381). Under these conditions, painting might remain relevant to Williams's poetry on the basis of self-referentiality, but it would not be relevant on the basis of materiality, physical sensation, the other dimension that I have claimed to be essential to Williams's "ethics of painting."

Because he took both of these dimensions of painting into consideration as he extracted lessons for poetry, Williams was able, on the one hand, to anticipate much of the post-structuralist critique of symbolism, while, on the other hand, he could conceive an alternative to that violence that post-structuralism regards as inescapable. "Violence is the human and transhuman law," Miller finally concedes in *The Linguistic Moment* (*LM* 336), having traversed a considerable distance since he identified Williams with an art of "calm description." In the course of that journey, Miller has advanced our understanding of Williams by revealing the element of interpretation that lies at the heart of the kind of description Williams practiced. But Miller has betrayed the ethical motive he earlier attached to description, the "heart" of describing in another sense. I press on that term, in a spirit of play I believe to be in keeping with Williams's attitude toward language, to evoke the "art of describing" as Svetlana Alpers has lately defined it in seventeenth-century Dutch painting (*AD*). Because Alpers appears to share the goals that originally united Williams and Miller, her example supports my sense of a general critical climate operating on a variety of fronts. But because Alpers is primarily concerned with the art of painting, her example suggests the role that painting might play in formulating the alternative to Miller's conclusions that I believe Williams still offers.

The position that Miller assigns to Williams is similar to the position that Alpers assigns to the sixteenth-century Flemish artist Peter Brueghel, whose affinity with Williams was recognized by the poet himself in a series of poems that includes the principal texts examined in this book.[9] Each artist turns his respective art toward "reality," taken in a sense that both Miller and Alpers are careful to distinguish from the positivism associated with the nineteenth century.[10] The artist does not merely record a world from which he stands apart but rather conveys his experience of being a part of a world, among the trees and stones, as Williams put it, or among the peasants, as some of Brueghel's best known paintings declare—though of course in neither case would it be fair to infer that the artist is claiming to *be* a stone or a peasant. He interprets the objects he describes, but as O'Hara argued in the case of Pollock, this sort of interpretation, eschewing appropriation, restores the object to itself. Thus, Alpers argues, "a study of the motif of the dance in Bruegel's paintings would show I think that he uses it less as a symbol of sin than as an image of the way the world is" (BFP 168n18; see fig. 2). The opposition to symbolism that Alpers shares with Miller is specifically directed against the tradition of reading Brueghel's paintings as moral allegories. "We are dealing not with moral views that are translated into art," Alpers suggests, "but with something that perhaps art alone can do" (BFP 176). The artistic act itself, in establishing a relation between artist and object, is an ethical act.

Nevertheless, as long as the object seems impersonal, merely a representative of the world of things, the artist may appear to be engaged in an epistemological exercise, as Miller and frequently even Alpers (SK) portray it. Ethical questions are more likely to appear primary when the "object" is a person, particularly a female person under the gaze of a male observer, a conventional arrangement in Western painting. Influenced by the concerns of feminist criticism, Alpers draws a distinction in the handling of this arrangement between the "classic" southern or Italian mode and the northern mode that she identifies with the "art of describing." Dürer's illustration of perspective practice (fig. 3) represents the former mode, although in the work of a northern artist. "The attitude toward women in this art," Alpers observes, "is part and parcel of a commanding attitude taken toward the possession of the world."[11] In the art of Vermeer (fig. 4), on the other hand,

> women are a world apart, inviolate, self-contained, but more significantly, self-possessed. These are works in which the quality of the paint (that intangible nature of the painted points of light) and the quality of rendering (the poise of the weighty figures) engage human implications [or what I would call ethical implications] that are rare in Dutch art. Vermeer recognizes the world present in these women as something that is other than himself, and with a kind of passionate detachment he lets it, through them, be.[12]

The emphasis on detachment in this account may make it appear that Alpers's version of "letting things be" is very different from the version, based on the artist's sense of being at one with things, that Miller describes in *Poets of Reality*. It seems likely, however, that Alpers would want to ascribe to Vermeer's relation to women, at the end of a tradition (*AD* 118), the same complex structure that she ascribes to Brueghel's relations to peasants, at the beginning of the tradition. "Bruegel is playing a kind of game—drawing us in and letting us also feel, simultaneously, that we are separate," Alpers explains (BFP 174). So too, if Vermeer's position is one of "detachment," it is at the same time "passionate." From Alpers's hints that the passion resides in "the quality of the paint," it is not too great a step to a hypothesis deducible from the psychoanalytic investigations of Julia Kristeva: that the artist has invested in his medium those energies that he might have invested in "possession" of the woman.[13] The same process that brings the paint to life lets the woman be.

This hypothesis suggests how the physical properties of the medium, highlighted not only in abstract expressionism but in the earlier art of Vermeer, may be implicated in the ethical position from which both Miller and Alpers set out. It also suggests why Alpers's focus on the art of painting may have permitted her to remain more faithful to that position than Miller has been. As I have formulated it, however, the hypothesis already oversteps the bounds of Alpers's explicit argument and ventures into a realm that I believe Williams explored in his art but only psychoanalysis has attempted to map. In my effort to follow Williams's exploration, I will make use especially of the map drawn by Julia Kristeva. The linguistic concerns that turned Miller toward deconstruction, the feminist concerns that surface in Alpers, and the psychoanalytic concerns that persuaded Williams to "accept all the help I can get from Freud's theory of the dream" (SE 281), all enter into Kristeva's project of building "a strong ethics, not normative but directed, which no transcendence guarantees" (KR 319).

Kristeva broadens the scope of linguistics by testing its assumptions against the example of painting, "something that is more-than-speech, a meaning to which space and color have been added" (DL 210). By focusing especially on the portrayal of the Virgin Mother in Western painting, Kristeva is able to examine the same issues that the "inviolate" women of Vermeer present to Alpers.[14] Kristeva's psychoanalytic perspective, however, challenges Alpers's conclusion that such figures, having escaped possession by the artist, remain in a state of self-possession. In Kristeva's ethics, possession in any form, though not finally erased, is continually displaced by an opposing force. The resulting dynamic is the condition that Kristeva calls love, an "exquisite mixture of destructive possession and idealization" (TL 61), very like the mixture that makes of "The whore and the virgin, an identity" (P 210), in the fifth book of Williams's long poem Paterson (1958).

Within that poem, the figure of the virgin-whore also brings together the poet Williams and the painter Brueghel, as Williams devotes a lengthy passage to a meditation on Brueghel's *The Adoration of the Kings* (1564), now in the National Gallery, London.[15] Since Williams's response to Brueghel's version of the Epiphany scene assembles all of the issues that I have just surveyed, I have chosen a character or set of characters from that scene as the starting point for each of the following chapters. The relation between the Baby and the Wise Men (chapters 2 and 3) raises the epistemological questions explored by Miller in *Poets of Reality*, specifically, the nature of the world to be known and the status of the knower. Since these questions provide the bridge by which Miller crosses over into deconstruction, the chapters I devote to them also provide an opportunity for examining the contribution of deconstructive criticism to our understanding of Williams. That contribution has been limited, in my view, by deconstruction's inability to conceive of an intersubjective relation that is not a violent struggle for possession. The Soldiers in Brueghel's Epiphany scene (chapter 4) furnish an occasion for exploring Williams's implication in such violence, and thus for turning from questions of epistemology to questions of ethics. Williams fully engages questions of ethics as he interprets the relation between Joseph and Mary, or the Old Man and the Virgin, as Williams calls them (chapters 5 and 6). It is a relation that displaces violence in a structure that Kristeva's study of love serves to illuminate.

To the extent that my concluding chapter reflects on a character from Brueghel's Epiphany scene, it is one who is not directly portrayed in the painting but stands in the foreground of Williams's account: Peter Brueghel himself, as a figure for the artist but also as a figure for the interpreter. Williams would seem to agree with Miller that any artistic practice performs an interpretive function. In this instance, Williams has devoted his art to a reading of Brueghel. Accordingly, the last chapter focuses on the implications of Williams's "ethics of painting" for the act of reading, a topic that runs throughout the preceding chapters, and that makes this as much a book about the ways in which Williams has been read as it is about Williams himself. Indeed, deconstruction seeks to demonstrate that criticism will always constitute an "allegory of reading" in this sense, since the reader's failure to capture any text "in itself" refocuses attention on the attempt at capture.[16] I will approach Williams's account of the marriage of Joseph and Mary as an allegory of reading, placing the partners in the marriage in the positions of reader and text. But I will permit the image of marriage to modify the image of the hunt, also present in *Paterson* 5, and the special object of Joseph Riddel's deconstructive reading.[17] Although, as Riddel demonstrates, Williams deconstructs the hunt, I will argue that he does not dissolve the marriage.

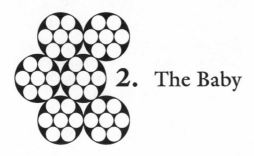

2. The Baby

IN THE LAST YEARS of his life William Carlos Williams wrote three poems treating the subject of the Epiphany, or the Adoration of the Magi, as presented by a work of visual art. The "old print" referred to in "The Gift" (1956; *CP2*: 430–31) cannot be securely identified, but Peter Brueghel's *Adoration of the Kings* (fig. 5) is the acknowledged visual source both for the opening lines of section 3 of *Paterson* 5 (1958; *P* 226–28) and the fourth poem of the sequence "Pictures from Brueghel" (1960; *CP2*: 387–88).[1] The three poems featuring the magi have a place in a larger series of Christmas poems, of which the best known is "Burning the Christmas Greens" (1944). The persistence with which Williams returns to the subject attests to its significance for him, yet its traditional significance makes its presence in Williams's work seem anomalous. "What right has Williams, a nonbeliever, to write such a poem?" That was how Williams himself expressed his doubts when he sent his poem "For Eleanor and Bill Monahan," addressed to the "Mother of God," to his Catholic friend Thomas Cole (Mariani, *NWN* 655).

Of course, from the standpoint of poetics rather than iconography, Williams's interest hardly seems anomalous. The sense that James Joyce assigned to the term "epiphany" has been widely applied to other writers whose work features the sudden radiance of a mundane object or occurrence when it comes into "exact focus."[2] Scholars such as M. H. Abrams have shown the role of Joyce's epiphany within a larger cultural movement toward the secularization of formerly religious concepts. Williams's retelling of the Christmas story might be understood merely as part of that process of secularization. However, critics who follow Hillis Miller's lead argue that Williams goes beyond the Romantic condition described by Abrams.[3] That condition, though secularized in its content, remains theological in its structure, insofar as it maintains a distinction between the radiant object and the meaning that radiates from it, the divine presence of traditional epiphany. Abrams acknowledges that a break from the Romantic tradition has occurred when "the traditional language is used . . . ironically, to identify phenomenal flare-ups that signify only themselves."[4] The intention appears less ironic if the literary practice is compared to the self-referentiality of modern painting, which Williams praised unequivocally.

As we have seen, Hillis Miller compared Williams's words to "splashes of paint on a canvas" when he sought to characterize Williams's post-Romantic position (*PR* 304), but in the same passage Miller slipped back into a theological comparison, that of "words as things incarnating their meanings." Although the two concepts meet in the scene of Christ's birth, that of incarnation might seem to represent a closer union between meaning and its vehicle than does the concept of epiphany, which requires some effacement of the vehicle to let the inner light shine forth. Logically, however, incarnation still assumes the prior existence of meaning in an ulterior, nonsensory world, from which the meaning descends into the image as body. The doctrine thus preserves the dualism that Miller hoped Williams had overcome. In fact, incarnation has increasingly come to be recognized as the theological counterpart of symbolist dualism and has become an object of the critique of symbolism discussed in the last chapter.[5]

Recent critics are likely to read Williams's Christmas poems in the context of this critique, though they by no means agree that it must take the deconstructive turn that Hillis Miller has given it. Thus, Paul Mariani, though far from employing the methods of deconstruction, nevertheless subscribes to some of its objectives in his summary of the issue that Williams engaged when he treated Brueghel's *Adoration* in *Paterson* 5: "Essentially, what was at issue here was that the icon, the symbol, the word, the logos, be returned to the fully human, and the symbolist or neo-symbolist poetic—with or without its Christian underpinnings—which underlies the practice of an Eliot or a Hart Crane (as well as a Baudelaire and even a Mallarmé) should be deprived of its logocentric, symbol-making connective" (*NWN* 709).

In the structure of the Epiphany scene, returning the logos to the fully human should have the effect of deemphasizing the centrality traditionally assigned to the incarnate Logos, the infant Christ, whose new, fully human status Williams signals by referring to him simply as "a Baby." Having accomplished this decentering, Williams proceeds to identify multiple centers in Brueghel's Epiphany, a procedure that

I have attempted to reflect in the chapter divisions of this book. Nevertheless, of the various centers that Williams identifies, it remains appropriate to consider the Baby first, because Williams strips him of one signifying function only to assign him a new one as a figure for the entire scene in which he appears.

Mariani hints at this function in a reformulation of his statement about returning the logos to the fully human. The Brueghel passage in *Paterson* 5, Mariani concludes, implies "a poetic that should then return the world to men and women" (*NWN* 709). In this formulation, what returns is nothing less than "the world," and the birth of the Baby signifies that return. In a book entitled *William Carlos Williams: A New World Naked*, Mariani evidently intends to connect his reading of the "Baby / new born!" that "lies naked on his Mother's / knees," in *Paterson* 5, with the theme of "the new world of spring" (*NWN* 198) that Williams proclaimed in *Spring and All* (1923). That work is not only the source for Mariani's subtitle but also the starting point for the several new versions of Williams that have grown out of the work of Hillis Miller.[6]

Spring and All proceeds from the premise that ordinary experience is not experience of the world but rather of some form of barrier to "immediate contact with the world" (*CP1*: 177). The purpose of genuine art is to remove the barrier. Thus, in the Adoration scene the barrier takes the form of religious myth, according to Mariani. In their role as artists, Brueghel and Williams have "demythologized" the scene: "What Brueghel has given us, Williams says, is simply (and gloriously) a pretty peasant girl holding a baby—naked—upon her lap, serene, at peace, while all about the mother and child the scene bustles with life" (*NWN* 708). The glory of the presentation lies in the freshness of its perception, which is not limited to the one fresh object, the newborn Baby, but suffuses the entire scene that lies "all about." In like fashion, the arrival of spring is not just an event in the world but is itself the arrival of a new world, of spring *and all*. Finally, then, Williams does not merely critique the myth of incarnation but rewrites the myth in his own terms. Rather than celebrating the descent of spirit into the world from some superior realm, he celebrates the rising up of the world from concealment into nakedness.

This world poses problems of knowledge and interpretation that have divided critics into hostile camps over the past two decades. There is agreement that traditional metaphysical or symbolist definitions do not apply to such a world, but there is sharp disagreement about what definition does apply. For the remainder of this chapter, I will explore three definitions, representing positions that I will designate as the "naturalist," the "phenomenological," and the "deconstructionist." My aim is not to establish any one position as correct but rather to expose the complexity of Williams's poetry by showing how all three positions are mutually implicated in it. If my account appears at this stage to favor the deconstructionist position, that will be due largely to deconstruction's superior ability to tolerate such mutual implication. Eventually I hope to distinguish Williams's position from that of deconstruction by showing Williams to be yet more tolerant.

The "naturalist" position is the logical place to start an examination of contemporary views of Williams, because it is the position that most readers associate with Williams, and it has the longest history, going back at least to Kenneth Burke's assertion, in 1922, that Williams's poetics reduces to the relationship between "the eye" and "the thing upon which that eye alights."[7] In the view of his admirers, Williams has stripped that relationship of the religious associations that it retained in Romanticism. Williams's nature is not the dwelling place of spirit. It is the field, rather, of impersonal natural forces, such as those that drive the cycle of the seasons and that generate babies, and it has its conceptual origin later in the nineteenth century than Romanticism, in the biology of Charles Darwin. "Darwin / opened our eyes / to the gardens of the world," according to Williams in "Asphodel, That Greeny Flower."[8] In *Paterson* 5, which originated in the same project as "Asphodel," Brueghel can be taken as a Darwinian naturalist, offering another lesson in using the eyes, though in his case they scrutinize the "nature" constituted by human society:

> —it is a scene, authentic
> enough, to be witnessed frequently
> among the poor (I salute
> the man Brueghel who painted
> what he saw—

It is not merely Brueghel's eye that *Paterson* 5 celebrates, however. What appears to be the earliest surviving draft of the passage concludes by drawing attention to "the brain of a Brugel," the brain being defined as "what is behind the eyes / to guide them" (Yale). Too exclusive an emphasis on the role of the eye in Williams's poetics can distort the poet's sophisticated naturalism into the "realism" that Paul Mariani attributes to the bystanders in Brueghel's painting, who appear to be "too much the realists to be taken in by all this talk about a virgin birth" (*NWN* 708). It may well be that the virgin birth has been called into question by the man whom Brueghel portrays as whispering into Joseph's ear, but it is the question itself that thus acquires the pejorative connotations of "talk."[9] The medium of vision that Brueghel employs links him, according to Williams, not to the "vulgar soldiery" but to the magi, who "saw with their proper eyes."

The vision of the magi, the blindness of the soldiers, the displacement of Joseph, and the virginity of Mary are issues to be explored more fully in later chapters. Since my focus at the moment is on the Baby, as synecdoche for the new world appearing with all the freshness of spring, it seems worth considering what can be learned about that world by its opposition to language, a feature of Mariani's reading that seems entirely justified. The opposition is clearly announced in the opening lines of the Brueghel passage in *Paterson* 5:

> Peter Brueghel, the elder, painted
> a Nativity, painted a Baby
> new born!
> among the words.

As soon as he has stated this theme, Williams proceeds to develop the threatening nature of the surrounding words through a series of parallel epithets assigned to the attendant soldiers, who are both "savagely armed" and "whispering," that is, armed also with words.

The hostility of words emerges as a motif of *Paterson* early in the poem's composition. Book 2 (1948) portrays a female figure "lost among the words" (*P* 84). A draft for the opening of the third section of book 3 (1949) heightens the sense of entrapment associated with that condition:

> It is among the words that the fish swim,
> among the words; among the words—the history
>
> lies caught , ensnared at the head of the
> V shaped weir a crude mesh of twigs at the top   (Yale)

Although this language did not survive in the published version, the idea persists in an analogy between the rising flood of the river and the suffocating proliferation of texts:

> Texts mount and complicate them-
> selves, lead to further texts and those
> to synopses, digests and emendations.   (*P* 130)

If words thus compose a barrier to the "immediate contact with the world" proposed in *Spring and All*, such contact might be established through the senses, particularly the sense of sight. The scrupulous observation practiced by the naturalist can be invoked as a model once again, but Michel Foucault reminds us that in this respect the practice thus far identified with Darwin has a long prior history, extending back to the seventeenth century. The "almost exclusive privilege" granted to sight in the new natural history of "the Classical age," as Foucault calls it, requires a removal of the verbal accretions that attached themselves to the natural object in preceding ages.[10] Once that operation is performed, the natural world presents itself in that naked immediacy in which the Baby presents himself in Williams's poem. According to Foucault, "the words that have been interwoven in the very being of the beast have been unravelled and removed: and the living being, in its anatomy, its form, its habits, its birth and death, appears as though stripped naked" (129). In the culture of the seventeenth-century Netherlands, Svetlana Alpers finds imagery that corroborates Foucault (SK 159) and again appears to anticipate Williams. Alpers cites an account of the camera obscura by Constantijn Huygens, who "argues that such a picture cast on the wall of his room [as in a camera obscura] not only brings the 'truth new born into the clarity of the light of high noon' but that it also 'replaces all previous written histories of the world' " (SK 163). It thus appears to constitute a "natural" history in form as well as in content.[11]

Because she is concerned not only with vision but works of visual art, Alpers can help to focus attention on the role of such works in Williams's poetry, a role that my analysis thus far must seem to have overlooked. If Williams was interested in removing barriers to immediate contact with the world, as Mariani's reading emphasizes, why would he risk imposing a barrier of his own by inserting another art work between the world and his poem? Why, moreover, would he draw attention to that insertion with such insistence that Williams's Virgin, translated from Brueghel's painting, appears even to Mariani as an "icon" (*NWN* 708)?

To answer these objections, I do not need to reject Williams's claims to realism, but I do need to reject the definition of realism implied when Mariani assigns that term to the Soldiers' knowledge of reproductive biology. The knowledge that Williams celebrates in the biologist Darwin is not "natural" in this sense, with respect to its object; concerned with "gardens," its object is as much an artificial construction as Foucault shows the world of the seventeenth-century naturalists to have been. Darwin's knowledge is "natural," however, insofar as the mind's capacity for artificial construction is the most "natural" human trait. According to *Spring and All*, "the only world of reality that men know [is] the world of the imagination, wholly our own" (*CP1*: 215).

This is the world known to phenomenology, which is not concerned with a "reality" existing apart from consciousness. Art is an activity of consciousness; indeed, it is the supreme activity of that heightened consciousness that Williams calls the imagination. A work of art, therefore, so far from presenting a barrier to the experience of the world, is the site in which the world is most likely to rise up in all its freshness. If this is the event to which Williams bears witness in Brueghel's painting, as a phenomenological reading of Williams would conclude, it would be an oversimplification to appeal to the quality of "naturalness" to distinguish the Baby who provides the event with its focus. In Williams's account, the Baby appears not only *in* a picture, but *as* a picture, "as from an / illustrated catalogue / in colors." To avoid reducing such an image to the status of a mere symbol, a vehicle for a meaning that lies elsewhere (for instance, in "nature"), the phenomenologist would insist on its quality of "presence."

By referring to "the phenomenologist," I intend to designate an attitude toward experience similar to the one adopted in the philosophical school known as phenomenology, but the attitude need not have been acquired through training in that school. It is remarkable, nevertheless, that the use of the term "presence" often signals the attitude, regardless of its origin. Critics from a variety of theoretical backgrounds have found the term applicable to Williams, and Williams himself employs it, notably in a passage in his *Autobiography* that bears directly on the Baby in the Adoration scene.[12] In the speech of his patients, Williams writes, the physician is able to detect a "rare presence," an "essence," "hidden under the verbiage, seeking to be realized."

Clearly, this is the drama of the Baby born "among the words," an analogy that is clinched by Williams's use of birth imagery in the same passage in the *Autobiography*. Here, however, that imagery does not permit the clear demarcation between the visual and the verbal suggested by the analogies I have noted from Foucault and Alpers. The demarcation in the *Autobiography* is drawn between "verbiage," which hides the "presence," and "words," which become present:

"The physician enjoys a wonderful opportunity actually to witness the words being born." "Verbiage" is language that has gone stale, while the "presence" of "words" consists in "their unspoiled newness." Lest we now suspect that the visual plays no part in this drama, Williams proceeds to describe "the words" in visual terms: "Their actual colors and shapes are laid before him. . . . He may see the difficulty with which they have been born and what they are destined to do." Even among these visual terms, a linguistic component may be discriminated from a more "purely" visual one. "Pure" seeing is involved in the perception of "actual colors and shapes." On the other hand, seeing into destiny, the kind of activity that distinguishes the magi from the uncomprehending Soldiers in the Adoration scene, is more visionary than visual. Since it involves the interpretation of signs, it might be called reading. Williams typically interweaves these two activities. "I myself invite you to read and to see," he declares at the outset of *Spring and All* (*CP1*: 178).

In contrast to Williams's practice, phenomenological criticism has attempted to unravel the separate threads of reading and seeing, assigning the privilege of "presence" to one or the other. According to Svetlana Alpers, "Pictorial representations do not signify; they make something present to sight" (SK 153). Consequently, the uncovering of "presence" in Dutch art does not entail reading: "The issue . . . is not reading and interpretation, but seeing and knowing" (SK 168). According to Hillis Miller, the issue is exactly the opposite in Williams's poetry, so it must be distinguished from painting, especially painting in the nonreferential, nonsignifying, abstract mode. Williams, according to Miller, "has none of that tormenting fear of reference which haunts modern art, no desire to abolish the naming power of words in order to create a poem which will be entirely free of objects, like an abstract painting" (*PR* 305). Miller finds "the naming power of words" to be the guiding principle of *Spring and All*, in which Williams asserts, "The only means [the poet] has to give value to life is to recognize it with the imagination and name it; this is so" (*CP1*: 202; *Daedalus* 422). The value thus produced is, in Miller's terms, "the supreme value of presence and of the present" (*Daedalus* 417).

"In such a way does one permit oneself to see without reading, to read without seeing," remarks Jacques Derrida, commenting on the method of another phenomenologist, Martin Heidegger.[13] Rather than offering a distinct alternative to the two positions thus far examined, the naturalist and the phenomenological, deconstruction, as practiced by Derrida, questions whether those two positions are any more distinct from each other than the two practices of seeing and reading in which their debates are continually entangled. For example, Derrida's extended examination of the treatment of a painting by Van Gogh in Heidegger's "Origin of the Work of Art" hinges on the juxtapositon of the two questions, "Are we reading? Are we looking?"[14] However, in the most influential application of deconstruction to the work of Williams, Hillis Miller has carried over from his earlier phenomenological orientation a distrust of the sense of sight as disruptive of immediacy (*PR* 312; *LM* 362–63). What deconstruction has changed for Miller is his understanding of immediacy, at first virtually a synonymn for "presence," but now associated with "a kind of non-present, interrupting ever so slightly the presence of the words on the page" (*LM* 387). Miller calls this interruption "the linguistic moment," and he identifies it with the "act of naming" that he had earlier analyzed in *Spring and All* (*LM* 375). Accordingly, this "act of naming," rather than the double act of reading and seeing, will afford readier access to the deconstructive dimension in Williams's treatment of the Baby.

Deconstruction regards the act of naming itself as a double act, whose components, analogous to seeing and reading, are the "proper name" and metaphor. "A noun is proper when it has but a single sense," Derrida explains in "White Mythology."[15] This is the ideal of philosophy—even, according to Derrida, the ideal that *is* philosophy. Its relation to seeing is pragmatically demonstrated in Svetlana Alpers's discussion of Dutch educational philosophy, in which words and pictures both function as names, insofar as names refer unambiguously to things in "the real world" (*AD* 96). Because the pictures that concern Alpers do not eschew reference, they participate in the same equation, "to name is to describe" (*AD* 98), in which Miller, in *Poets of Reality*, inserts Williams's poetry: "an art which is calm description, naming one by one [because the "proper" noun has a "single sense"] the visible and tangible qualities of an object" (*PR* 305).

To account for *Spring and All*, however, Miller finds it necessary to separate naming, which Williams celebrates, from description, which Williams denigrates. "In description," Williams explains, "words adhere to certain objects, and have the effect on the sense of oysters, or barnacles" (*CP1*: 234). In contrast, as Miller extends the argument, "naming frees words from such adhesion to become independent energies with which the poet creates a new object—the poem" (*Daedalus* 425). In this mode of "imaginative naming," then, the bond between word and thing that secures the "proper" name is broken, resulting in the freedom of metaphor, which, in Aristotle's classic definition, transfers the name of one thing to something else.[16]

In contrast to his previous emphasis on Williams's avoidance of figurative language (*Views* 4), the major role that Miller assigns to figural play in his 1970 essay on *Spring and All* reflects his new interest in Derrida, whose study of metaphor in Aristotle's philosophy Miller acknowledges (*Daedalus* 433 n45). But Miller had read *Spring and All* before he had read Derrida, and he had long been struggling to find a conceptual framework that could accommodate, on the one hand, Williams's pronouncements about imaginative freedom, and on the other hand, the sense of transparent objectivity produced by his poems. The importance to Miller of Derrida is most apparent in Miller's revision of that framework. At first, Miller claimed that Williams had found a way to transcend two positions continually alternating in the history of Western art. Williams "rejects both the mirror and the lamp, both the classical theory of art as imitation, and the romantic theory of art as transformation" (*PR* 309–10), both "proper" and metaphoric naming, in other words. Later, following Derrida's exposition of the interdependency of both types of naming in Aristotle, Miller concedes that, "like Aristotle's *mimesis*, Williams' imagination is both part of and more than nature, both immediate and mediatorial. . . . Like the long tradition he echoes, Williams remains caught in the inextricable web of connection among these concepts" (*Daedalus* 429).

Along with Williams, painting and poetry, too, are caught in that web, no less inextricably. To Joseph Riddel, who goes further than Miller in deconstructing the interrelationship between poetry and painting, "their entanglement . . . is not simply analogy, but a figure of the doubleness of figuration itself. The irreducibility of one to the other, or the play between what might be called the metaphorical and literal, or even the figural and referential," or, in Derrida's terms, the metaphorical and the "proper," "characterizes what Williams will later celebrate as the volatility of language" (*Glyph* 207). That volatility acquires literal force in a famous figure from *Spring and All* that features prominently in the analyses of both Riddel and Miller: "As birds' wings beat the solid air without which none could fly so words freed by the imagination affirm reality by their flight."[17] Such words, "freed by the imagination" from the bondage required of "proper" names, are tropes or figures of speech. The "doubleness of figuration" to which Riddel refers is pictured in Williams's image of troping as a movement away from yet simultaneously toward reality. In contrast to our "common sense" notion of metaphor, in which the figurative sense acquires its concreteness from the literal sense, in Williams's formulation it is the figurative that gives firmness to, "af-firms," the literal.

In "The Gift," the first of Williams's Adoration poems to make explicit reference to a work of visual art, something very similar to the flight of the birds in *Spring and All* is imaged in the flight of devils from the advent of the divine. That flight, too, is an affirmation: "The very devils / by their flight give praise." No doubt we could say the same of the "whispering men" who turn from the Baby "with averted faces" in the Adoration scene in *Paterson* 5, and thereby get "to the heart / of the matter" even as they misconstrue its nature. The Baby, then, would be the reality that is affirmed by figurative flight. If one accepts up to this point, however, the unusual perspective that Williams seems to be offering, one cannot rest content merely with designating the fixed position of the Baby as "real" or literal, and the turning of the bystanders as "imaginary" or figural, or appealing to some other neat polarity, such as that between painting and poetry. The operation that Williams is performing has the effect of radically unsettling any such stability. Once the traditional relationship between the literal and figural is inverted, their separation cannot be maintained. They continually reappear, one "reinscribed," as the deconstructionists say, in the other.

Such reinscription is evident in Williams's presentation of the Baby "as from an / illustrated catalogue / in colors." At first this image seems to reinforce a division of Brueghel's painting along lines already suggested: on the one hand a verbal realm, that of the whispering bystanders; on the other hand a specially visual realm, that of the Baby. The specification of "colors," a feature also of the passage from Williams's *Autobiography* examined earlier, highlights a quality often emphasized by those who would argue that visual art captures phenomenological "presence" in a way that resists verbal analysis.[18] However, such resistance would seem to have been overcome in the case of an image from "an illustrated catalogue." By means of that specification, a verbal element is reinscribed within the visual domain of the Baby, and the visual reappears in turn as a captive of the verbal. As Wendy Steiner says of illustrations, in terms that seem to echo Williams, "they appear to entrap the thing-world among words."[19]

This chapter's progression in defining the Baby, first as "nature," then as "picture," is paralleled by Steiner's further observation concerning illustrations, that what appears as the "thing-world" is "in fact—or in addition" the "pictorial world." Whereas symbolism separates these worlds, with the symbol, over here, standing for the meaning, over there, phenomenology infuses "picture" with thinglike "presence." From phenomenology, deconstruction inherits this infusion, but it also accepts the logical distinction drawn by symbolism. Infusion becomes infection. The literalism that Alpers can comfortably associate with pictorial representations becomes simultaneously, and irreconcilably, figurative.

If one must have a term to designate the definition of the Baby that emerges from deconstructive analysis, the rhetorical term *catachresis* may be the most appropriate. It seems forbiddingly foreign, but then so do the patterns of thought that deconstruction seeks to introduce. Catachresis is the term through which Hillis Miller establishes the link between his study of "the linguistic moment," in a series of poets including Williams, and Derrida's study of the place of metaphor in philosophy. As Miller explains (*LM* 330, 335), catachresis, in deconstructive analysis, is understood as that rhetorical figure which is simultaneously literal and figurative. It is a name transferred from elsewhere, and is thus figurative; but it functions as a literal or "proper" name because it applies to what otherwise would have no name. The very mobility of this chapter's search for a name, from "nature" to "picture" to "catachresis," suggests the ultimately nameless condition of that thing Williams names the Baby.

Although Williams himself did not use the term catachresis, his prose demonstrates a full awareness of what is involved in that term for deconstructionists. In this case, the prose does not come from *Spring and All* but from a work of the same period, a "Comment" that Williams wrote for the second issue of the magazine *Contact* in January 1921.[20] No doubt referring to the installments of *Ulysses* that he had been reading as they appeared in the *Little Review* (Mariani, *NWN* 149), Williams observes that Joyce "is following some unapparent sequence quite apart from the usual syntactical one." Further on, he reasserts the idea of "freedom . . . from usage" as a distinguishing feature of Joyce's method. Deliberate violation of the rules of usage for rhetorical effect is a traditional definition of catachresis.[21]

The implications that deconstruction draws from this procedure are worked through in an image that Williams inserts into his analysis. Joyce demands, according to Williams, that the reader "separate the words from the printed page, to take them up into a world where the imagination is at play and where the words are no more than titles under the illustrations." The ascending movement and the play of the imagination link this image to the image of figuration as the flight of birds in *Spring and All*. The contrast of words and illustrations links it further to the interplay of the verbal and the visual in the presentation of Brueghel's Baby in *Paterson* 5. In the passage from *Contact*, however, the instability of that interplay is emphasized even more. We think we are following words in their ascent, as in the image of birds, but once the ascent is accomplished, the words have somehow *become* illustrations; yet simultaneously, words are also present as words, in the debased role of mere titles. Once again, as in *Spring and All*, Williams demonstrates the "doubleness of figuration" revealed by deconstruction. But in this case there can be no mistake that what *Spring and All* calls "reality" is both established by figural play and is itself figural, a system of "illustrations."

Having noted thus far the affinity between Williams's understanding of what he was about and the understanding offered by deconstruction, I do not want to leave the passage from *Contact*, and the subject of the Baby, before noting one point of divergence that will become increasingly important as I pursue other features of the Epiphany scene. From the traditional analysis of catachresis, deconstruction inherits an image of violence that seems inevitably involved in the violation of usage. Williams affords an opportunity to question that inevitability. To be sure, just as Derrida summarizes one definition of catachresis as "the violent, forced, abusive inscription of a sign," so Williams states that Joyce "forces" him to follow the aberrant turns of his syntax.[22] But the impression left by "a world where the imagination is at play" is decidedly pastoral, somehow beyond "the use of force," which Williams duly acknowledges in his short story of that title (*FD* 131–35). In Williams's comment on Joyce, analogy with a "stroke of sunlight," not a stroke of lightning, heightens the peaceful impression of the force that Williams has in mind.

The guiding spirit of the *Contact* "Comment" is St. Francis of Assisi, whom Williams proposes making "the patron saint of the United States." Williams is particularly interested in the legend of St. Francis talking to the animals, a practice that must have required considerable forcing of language out of its conventional patterns but did not force the "natural" patterns of the audience, according to Williams: "Nor do I think it is especially recorded that St. Francis tried to make the sparrows Christians. When the service was over each beast returned to his former habits." Before we seek to make Williams a deconstructionist, we would do well to meditate on the example of St. Francis.[23]

3. The Wise Men

IN THE FOURTH ISSUE of *Contact* (Summer 1921), Williams pursued his campaign for St. Francis by presenting the saint as a wise man, or rather, a wise man as the saint. He is "St. Francis Einstein of the Daffodils," in the poem of that title, which Williams wrote to celebrate Albert Einstein's first visit to the United States. That visit continued a long procession of European masters whose presence on Williams's native ground seemed to pose as much a threat as a stimulus, especially when they exercised their mastery in the area of the arts. Within that area, Williams's ambivalence toward Marcel Duchamp and André Breton, as masters of Dada and surrealism respectively, represents Williams's response to two successive waves of European immigration, occasioned by this century's two world wars.[1] Chronologically, Williams's treatment of the biblical Wise Men in the series of poems on which I am focusing reflects his response to the second wave, but it has roots in the earlier period, just as surrealism has roots in Dada.

At both moments, Williams attempts a conjunction of Einstein and St. Francis: first in the Dadaesque poem "St. Francis Einstein of the Daffodils"; later in Williams's manifesto for the aborted surrealist magazine *Midas*.[2] Involved in that conjunction are two strategies that Williams typically employed to defuse the threat of alien mastery. One strategy was to undermine the traditional foundation of mastery by declaring, as Williams does in "St. Francis Einstein," "Oldfashioned knowledge is / dead under the blossoming peachtrees."[3] Another strategy was to attend to that blossoming, to discover in the old foundation's "decomposition," as Williams calls it in another *Contact* comment (December 1920; *RI* 66), a new space that all could share. Thus, Williams transforms Einstein's theory of relativity into the lesson "that flowers and men / were created / relatively equal" (*CP1*: 131), just as St. Francis "mingled with the animals as an equal" (*SE*

27), by virtue of that "common language" (*SE* 29) whose rediscovery became the problem Williams posed to himself in *Paterson* (*P* 7) and in his controversial quest for a "new measure" for poetry.[4] The heart of the problem was that commonality must not erase difference; relativity had to be preserved amid equality. When St. Francis communes with the animals, "the lion roars and the ass brays" (*SE* 28). Similarly, when the Wise Men visit the stable in the poem "The Gift," "The ass brayed / the cattle lowed." It is a Franciscan scene.

Of Williams's several poems on the Epiphany, "The Gift" does most to highlight the question of knowledge, first by introducing "the wise men of old" in the first line, and then by repeating a form of the verb "to know" four times in the next twenty-five lines, the first half of the poem. Lack of knowledge threatens to block effective communication between the so-called Wise Men and the Baby they have come to honor:

> What could a baby know
>   of gold ornaments
> or frankincense and myrrh,
>   of priestly robes
>   and devout genuflections?

The Baby is not alone in its ignorance, however:

> The men were old
>   how could they know
> of a mother's needs
>   or a child's
>   appetite?

Situated at the opposite extremes of youth and age, the Baby and the Wise Men test the limits of a common language. The gifts that constitute their medium of exchange are bound to seem "unsuitable," as the first half of the poem declares them to be. Yet the second half of the poem affirms the gifts to be fully adequate both to "a mother's needs" (for love) and "a child's appetite" (for milk).

The boldness of that affirmation can be better appreciated if it is first determined how far Williams was willing to push his claims for the "unsuitability" of the conditions from which the affirmation emerges. In his treatment of Brueghel's *Adoration* in *Paterson* 5, Williams suggests not that the gifts of the Wise Men fail to meet legitimate demands but that the gifts are themselves illegitimate, or improper:

> But the gifts! (works of art,
> where could they have picked
> them up or more properly
> have stolen them?)

A superficial reading of this passage would allow "properly" to modify "stolen," as if there could be such a thing as a proper theft.[5] Of course, the rational explanation for this confusion is that "properly" does not modify "stolen" but rather the elided verb "to speak," which, if restored, would yield the phrase, "to speak more properly." So far from encouraging confusion, then, Williams presents himself as carefully discriminating among his terms: as a term, compared to "picked up," "stolen" is the more proper designation for the improper act that Williams imagines the Wise Men to have performed. However, in another passage, noted in the preceding chapter, the term "proper" unmistakably refers to another act performed by the Wise Men: they "saw with their proper eyes." The conflict between these two uses of the term "proper" makes it very difficult to determine just how Williams intends to characterize the Wise Men and arouses the suspicion that, despite his declared intention, Williams is not "speaking properly" at all.

In fact, throughout the Brueghel passage in *Paterson* 5, Williams performs a deconstruction of the notion of the "proper" similar to Derrida's analysis of the "proper name" applied to Williams in the preceding chapter. Williams's inability to characterize the Wise Men definitively is a direct consequence of such analysis. In the first place, unless words are employed in their "proper" sense, the act of definition itself becomes impossible. As Aristotle argues in a passage from the *Metaphysics* quoted by Derrida in "White Mythology," "not to have one meaning is to have no meaning, and if words have no meaning, reasoning with other people, and indeed with oneself, has been annihilated."[6] But if reasoning is annihilated, the possibility of knowledge is destroyed along with it. It therefore becomes impossible to say not only that *these* men are Wise Men, but that any men can be wise—unless, of course, Williams intends to propose some ground for wisdom other than knowledge, or to propose a wisdom that functions without a ground.

Not surprisingly, in *Paterson* 5 Williams does not use the name "Wise Men." Instead, he moves through a series of provisional names, much as the preceding chapter moved through a series of attempted definitions of the Baby, whose "proper name," also, Williams avoids. The grammatical indeterminacy that has only been sampled so far can be felt in its cumulative force in the series of disjointed phrases applied to the Wise Men, as I will continue to call them for lack of a better term whose absence Williams seeks to reveal:

> The crowned and mitred heads
> of the 3 men, one of them black,
> who had come, obviously from afar
> (highwaymen?)
> by the rich robes
> they had on—offered
> to propitiate their gods[7]

A line of white space follows before we are told "Their hands were loaded with gifts." Logically, the gifts are what these men offer "to propitiate their gods," whose plural number seems to reflect the multiplication of meanings at work in this passage generally. Grammatically, the offering might just as well be the men's heads, which stand at the "head" of the passage, in the position normally reserved for the grammatical subject. If the verb "offered" does not convey decapitation semantically, it must suffer decapitation syntactically. Nor can we stabilize this language by appealing to its supposed referent, the picture that it purports to describe. Of Brueghel's three kings, only the black king at the right wears anything on his head, and that headband with projecting spikes only distantly resembles a crown or miter. The central, eldest king has laid his crown on the ground, producing a visual dislocation that echoes the operation of Williams's grammar.[8]

If not the painting, the painter, finally, offers some hope of terminating analysis. In the *Paterson* passage, "Brueghel" is the only proper name that Williams employs, three or four times, depending on where we determine the passage to end. A charitable reading might explain the series of lines beginning with "The crowned and mitred heads" as a collection of observations by "the man Brueghel who painted / what he saw," as Williams declares four lines earlier. Moreover, the very feature that seems to instigate the multiplication of meanings for Williams, the "improper" appearance of the three kings, can be explained as the result of Brueghel's effort to maintain his unique identity.

In the study that set the agenda for modern interpretations of this painting, Max Dvořák argued that the peasant awkwardness displayed in all of the figures was Brueghel's way of keeping his distance from the idealizing spirit of Italian art, to which, in matters of composition, Brueghel comes unusually close in this case. The vertical format, the relatively large size of the figures, their unification by means of a system of crisscrossing diagonals, are all elements that Dvořák links to Italian art. But "the Italianate Madonna has here been transformed into a Flemish peasant girl, the Magi look like exotically clad participants in a Christmas procession, and St. Joseph stands in both physical and spiritual proximity to the surrounding crowd."[9] In connecting the magi with a Christmas procession, Dvořák alludes to what many art historians regard as the source for paintings of the *Adoration of the Magi* in Brueghel's time: the processions in celebration of the Feast of the Epiphany, in which local townspeople would represent the three kings.[10] Along with their gifts, these amateur actors had "stolen" their very identity.

Williams, who is likely to have known Dvořák's interpretation, may have found in it a possible solution to the problem of coming to terms with foreign influences, the problem that Williams's own "wise men from the east," the émigré artists and intellectuals, had forced him to confront.[11] In his second treatment of Brueghel's *Adoration*, for the "Pictures from Brueghel" sequence, Williams gave a central place to the issue of Brueghel's relation to Italian art. The various characters that Brueghel has assembled, Williams observes,

> make a scene copied we'll say
>
> from the Italian masters
> but with a difference

In that difference lies the secret of Brueghel's own mastery:

> the mastery
>
> of the painting
> and the mind the resourceful mind
> that governed the whole
>
> the alert mind dissatisfied with
> what it is asked to
> and cannot do

Here, for once, is an image of authority that Williams appears eager to endorse rather than overturn. So strong is the assertion of mastery that when Williams hints there might be something that this mind cannot do, the reader is quick to translate the deficiency into another gesture of potency. Presumably what Brueghel has been asked to do is to copy the Italian masters. One imagines him replying, "I cannot be other than myself." Caught up in such imagining, Robert Lawson-Peebles has recently revealed its logical outcome. Williams is held to have claimed for Brueghel that "above all, his mastery is absolute. In this respect, Bruegel emerges as the God that myth and religion cannot supply."[12]

Such a reading may reflect the ideal text of High Modernism, created ex nihilo by the artist, who withdraws from his universe, the autonomous artwork, once he has set it in motion. The particular text of Williams's poem, however, implies a different figure. However much Williams may claim for Brueghel's mastery, he does not claim that it is absolute. It is based on a difference, and the measure of that difference is internal to Brueghel's art, in the Italianate elements that Brueghel "copied," as Williams admits along with Dvořák. Later, toward the end of his poem, Williams states that Brueghel,

> accepted the story and painted
> it in the brilliant
> colors of the chronicler

The mind at work here is not "resourceful" in the sense of containing within itself a source of pure invention. Rather, it is "resourceful" in its ability to make do with available materials. "We can expect to invent nothing of our materials," Williams once stated flatly.[13] At the end of *Paterson* 5, he bestows the epithet "resourceful" on an old woman who inserts "a china doorknob / in her vagina to hold her womb up" (*P* 238).

Various passages throughout Williams's work similarly subvert the traditional meaning of other "master" terms that Williams applies to Brueghel. The ability to "govern" can be valued for the freedom it permits rather than the restraint it exercises, as when Williams advises the poet "to govern his sensibilities, his mind, his will so that it accord delicately with his emotions."[14] For a poet who had already urged himself, at the end of *Paterson* 4 (1951), to "Waken from . . . this dream of / the whole poem" (*P* 200), the "whole" that Brueghel's mind is said to govern would be constituted by the governor's lack of intervention, his acknowledgment of "a world detached from the necessity of recording it, sufficient to itself, removed from him" (*CP1*:

207). According to another of Williams's "Pictures from Brueghel," when Brueghel painted a wheat field, "it remained a wheat field" (*CP2*: 389), just as the animals to whom St. Francis preached remained animals. Yet it is doubtful that Williams, rejecting the godlike status that Lawson-Peebles would assign to Brueghel, would accept the saintlike status implied in a comparison with St. Francis. Brueghel's "resourcefulness" indicates that he belongs to the modern world that Williams describes in his *Contact* comment on St. Francis, a world in which "there is no genius [like St. Francis] who can make a sermon of understanding deep enough and gentleness of sufficient catholicity to include all our animals, birds and fishes" (*SE* 29). In the absence of such genius, artists can only "create their own imaginative world as best they can with what they have."

Though their means may be less adequate, modern artists have inherited the saints' responsibility: to "stand between man and nature as saints once stood between man and the sky," as Williams declares in *Spring and All* (*CP1*: 199). Hence, it is a serious distortion to view Williams as "secularizing and aestheticizing" religious myth, as critics such as Jerome Mazzaro (*LP* 154) and Lawson-Peebles have done. One consequence of that distortion is that it produces an impression of total adequacy—the artist as God—where Williams is struggling with a desperate sense of inadequacy. On at least one occasion, Williams had the opportunity to make the necessary correction himself. During an interview with Williams in 1952, Eli Siegel alluded to a scene in *A Voyage to Pagany* (1928) in which the autobiographical protagonist, Dev Evans, stares in amazement at a statue of Venus (*VP* 109–10). Siegel's intention was to discuss Williams's interest in sculpture, but Williams quickly responded, "that wasn't my feeling toward sculpture, it was my feeling toward Venus."[15] He went on to confess, "Of course I was in despair of ever seeing 'the god.' It is the thing that depresses me always."

Whenever Williams comes close to seeing the god, Venus is the god in question.[16] Even "St. Francis Einstein of the Daffodils" emerges from "Venusremembering wavelets" (*CP1*: 130). Thus, if Williams transforms the religious tenor of the Epiphany scene, the effect of that transformation is paganizing rather than secularizing. Mary is identified with Venus, mother of "the god of love," as Williams refers to the Baby both in "The Gift" and in *Paterson* 5 (*P* 233). The Wise Men in "The Gift" worship the "perfection" of the mother, just as Dev Evans worships the "perfection" of the Venus Anadyomene of Cyrene (*VP*

118; fig. 6). But Evans's belief that he has seen the god depends on "forgetting the stone, seeing a woman." In Williams's actual experience, the medium never achieved such transparency. While "the wise men of old" in "The Gift" may have witnessed perfection incarnate, in the modern perspective that dominates "Pictures from Brueghel" the artist can only represent the Virgin "as a work of art / for profound worship." Viewing art itself as a proper object for worship, as the aestheticizing reading would have it, overlooks Williams's insistence in *Paterson* that the gifts of the Wise Men, explicitly called "works of art," have been "stolen." Art substitutes for an unobtainable experience that Williams imagines to be more genuine. Even in "The Gift," where the Wise Men enjoy more mythical stature than in the poems based on Brueghel's painting, the gifts necessarily appear "unsuitable."

As I noted earlier, however, Williams gives "The Gift" a dramatic twist. As far as he extends his critique of the Wise Men's claim to knowledge—so far, in fact, that it extends to the artist's claim to mastery—Williams nevertheless credits their "unsuitable" gifts with an adequacy that is explicitly miraculous:

> A miracle
> had taken place,
>   hard gold to love,
> a mother's milk!
>   before
>   their wondering eyes.

If we search for an explanation of the miracle in the immediate context of these lines, we may be misled by Williams's use of the word "nature." By virtue of "their nature," Williams tells us, "The ass brayed / the cattle lowed," just as "All men by their nature give praise." From these statements it would be possible to deduce, first, the proposition that "all men" share a common human essence ("human nature"), and second, the proposition that men and animals share a common origin ("nature"). The commonality thus guaranteed by the concept of nature would provide the grounds for communication and perhaps even for the translation of hard gold to love.

However, such an interpretation would set the Wise Men of "The Gift" at odds with their counterparts in the poems based on Brueghel's painting. There, as I have indicated, rather than receiving their identity from nature, the Wise Men must steal both their identity and the gifts through which they communicate. Moreover, in another context that I have been applying, the legend of St. Francis as Williams presents it in his *Contact* comment, the example of the ass braying and the cattle lowing emphasizes the difference among the animals, and between animals and men, not their common nature. For Williams, the lack of a defining nature is the most "natural" characteristic of human beings: "It is the one outstanding human trait that we are unpredictable, variable" (*RI* 111). In "The Gift," variability is given maximum expression by the devils, who "by their flight give praise." The word "flight," with respect to the devils, stands in the same position as the word "nature," as Williams applies the formula to men.

In the preceding chapter, I discussed the flight of the devils in "The Gift" by analogy to the flight of the birds in *Spring and All*, which, in turn, represents for Williams the flight of "words freed by the imagination" (*CP1*: 235). "Imagination" seems a more likely name than "nature" for the force that presides at Williams's Epiphany scenes. The Brueghel passage in *Paterson* 5 declares that "the / imagination must be served," and "The Gift" reveals that

> the imagination
>   knows all stories
>   before they are told
> and knows the truth of this one
>   past all defection

This is the one passage in "The Gift" that uses the verb "to know" in a positive sense. Its presence offers reassurance that insofar as Williams is mounting a critique of knowledge, his purpose is not to deny the possibility of knowledge but to redefine what it means to have it, or perhaps precisely to deny the possibility of "having" it as a possession and the "mastery" that such possession entails. When Williams denies knowledge, he denies it to specific human agents: How can the Baby know? How can the Wise Men know? When he affirms knowledge, on the other hand, he removes human agency: "the imagination / knows."

The operation of the imagination in Shakespeare's work, as Williams analyzes it in *Spring and All*, helps illuminate the connection between the imagination and knowledge and simultaneously helps illustrate how difficult it is for Williams to dispel the impression of mastery when dealing with figures like Shakespeare, or, one might add, Brueghel. By reinterpreting the famous lines from *Hamlet* about art holding a mirror up to nature, Williams makes it clear that against the

Romantic tradition, he understands the imagination to be something separate from nature: "He [Shakespeare] holds no mirror up to nature but with his imagination rivals nature's composition with his own" (*CP1*: 208). The impression of mastery already begins to form here in the stamp of the possessive "his" placed on the imagination, just as knowledge becomes a possession a few paragraphs later. But the later passage denies possession in the same gesture that affirms it: "For S. to pretend to knowledge would have been ridiculous—no escape there—but that he possessed knowledge, and extraordinary knowledge, of the affairs which concerned him, as they concerned the others about him, was self-apparent to him" (*CP1*: 208–9). According to Williams, the knowledge to which Shakespeare could not pretend was the kind of knowledge that his rivals had acquired through university training. The kind of knowledge that Shakespeare possessed, on the other hand, is not, for Williams, merely knowledge based on observation of the world about him. This point deserves special emphasis because in the case of Williams's treatment of Brueghel, it would be similarly easy, and similarly erroneous, to assume that knowledge derives from simple observation. But at the outset of his analysis of Shakespeare in *Spring and All*, Williams emphatically declares that the writing he admires "is not a conscious recording of the day's experiences" (*CP1*: 207). To adopt such a goal would merely restore the subordination of writing to nature.

The kind of knowledge that Williams attributes to Shakespeare has its source in the imagination, as Williams declares at the outset of a paragraph in *Spring and All* so densely woven that it must be quoted in full:

> His [Shakespeare's] actual power was PURELY of the imagination. Not permitted to speak as W.S., in fact peculiarly barred from speaking so because of his lack of information, learning, not being able to rival his fellows in scientific training or adventure and at the same time being keen enough, imaginative enough, to know that there is no escape except in perfection, in excellence, in technical excellence—his buoyancy of imagination raised him NOT TO COPY them, not to holding the mirror up to them but to equal, to surpass them as a creater of knowledge, as a vigorous, living force above their heads. (*CP1*: 209)

This paragraph has the two-part structure already observed in "The Gift." At first, Williams emphasizes Shakespeare's inability; finally, however, he reaffirms his opening declaration of power. The two-part structure reflects two forms of agency, even as the first sentence is suspended between two forms of the possessive, "his" and "of the imagination." By the end, the power seems to belong to the man called Shakespeare. It is notable, however, that Williams begins his list of Shakespeare's inabilities with a denial of authorial voice, just as the first part of "The Gift" seems devoted to denying the personal agency of the Wise Men in the miracle that takes place. In *Spring and All,* even at the very end of the paragraph there is a degree of depersonalization in the transformation of Shakespeare into "a vigorous, living force." "Sometimes I speak of imagination as a force," Williams notes elsewhere in the same text (*CP1*: 235).

Whoever, or whatever, is "the creator of knowledge" that Williams locates in Shakespeare's texts, the introduction of the notion of creation in this context helps distinguish the type of knowledge that is distinctive of Shakespeare from that which he shares with his rivals. To be sure, little sharing is evident in the paragraph I have quoted, but a few lines earlier, Williams admits that Shakespeare had acquired forms from Marlowe and stories from "the common talk of his associates." Like Brueghel, then, Shakespeare copied the Renaissance masters, "but with a difference." The difference, in Shakespeare's case, lies in the second type of knowledge that his works bring into play. Unlike the knowledge that Shakespeare acquired from his rivals and that they acquired from the university, this second type of knowledge is not acquired, but rather produced. This is the sense in which "the imagination / knows all stories / before they are told"—as the producer of the stories, or "the structure of their telling," as Joseph Riddel puts it (*Glyph* 214).

An exploration of the mode of production involved here is necessary to substantiate my earlier claim that this type of knowledge is not available for possession. After all, if it is produced, the producer at least might be assumed to have a legitimate claim to possession. In the economy of Williams's Epiphany poems, however, possession only blocks production. Production begins when something is given away. In the terms of "The Gift," as long as the Wise Men retain their gold, it remains "unsuitable." Similarly, immediately after the Brueghel passage in *Paterson* 5, and the doubts it raises about Mary's chastity, Williams proclaims,

> no woman is virtuous
> who does not give herself to her lover
> —forthwith[17]

If a woman had written these words, one might be inclined to take them as evidence of a specially feminine relationship to the act of giving, such as Hélène Cixous has proposed.[18] Since a man wrote them, however, one is more likely to suspect them of urging the female beloved to give so that the male lover might possess. A full response to that criticism must await consideration of the figure of Joseph, as Williams portrays him in *Paterson* 5. It is worth raising the issue at this point, however, because it helps to throw light on the productivity of the Wise Men's gifts. If, as I have argued, Mary is the object of the Wise Men's worship in Williams's interpretation, then their gifts would be offered to her. Like Mary's giving of herself to her lover, the Wise Men perform an act of love by giving gold.

The connection between love and gold may have been suggested to Williams by the alchemical imagery of the surrealist Nicolas Calas, with whom Williams planned to launch the magazine *Midas*, named for the legendary king who could transform any substance into gold.[19] Love features prominently in Williams's manifesto for the magazine, when he praises a revolutionary poetry that "goes to the heart of human desire" (*RI* 160). He elaborates: "The one character of love which can be most respected by the poet is precisely that, the lavishing on the beloved of every gift in a man's power to lay at her feet," and the gift that he specifies is gold: "Love, as gold, its symbol, is most gold when it is given freely to the beloved" (*RI* 159).

In referring to gold as a symbol, Williams departs significantly from the traditional monetary theory in which gold possesses inherent value that is symbolized by money. Gold's signifying function is what matters to Williams, but his terminology obscures the nature of that function and lays gold open to the kind of attack that Williams himself directed against the symbol in literature. If gold were truly a symbol, it would represent something that already existed, as does the acquisitive knowledge associated with Shakespeare's rivals. A symbolic reading of "The Gift" would reverse the order of terms as Williams gives it, arguing that the miraculous transformation of "hard gold to love" simply "means" that love is symbolized by gold. In this reading, the gift economy is one of exchange, but Williams emphasizes production, as in the type of knowledge he attributes to Shakespeare. Gold brings into being that which it represents. In "The Gift," gold makes love. In "Midas," through being given away, gold makes its own identity, rather like Brueghel's "Wise Men in their stolen / splendor" (*CP2*: 387).

To find a designation other than "symbol" for the operation performed by Williams's gold, one might turn to modern linguistics for Saussure's definition of the "sign," or to Derrida's deconstruction of that linguistics, which would offer a variety of terms refusing to function as such, for example, "a becoming-sign of the symbol," or the simpler "trace."[20] However, since the status of terminology is so problematic in this line of thought, and since entering the debate over that status would only deflect our attention from Williams, I will refer only to one concept that does not name the operation in question but designates a crucial dimension of it: that of the materiality of the signifier. This is a dense formula, but a pair of phrases conjoined by Derrida succinctly represents what the concept meant for Saussure and how Derrida extends it: "The movement of signification adds something [Saussure], which results in the fact that there is always more [Derrida]."[21]

The difference between Derrida and Saussure on this issue corresponds to a difference between Williams and his lifelong friend and rival, Ezra Pound, in the area of economic theory.[22] In Pound's economics, the "something added" by the movement of signification is severely restricted. Although he seems to prefer a barter economy, Pound is willing to admit money, the movement of signification, as long as that movement adds no more than what is already present in the signified, the value of the goods represented by the money. Ideally, the three "natural categories" of transient, durable, and permanent goods should be represented by three different types of money that are correspondingly transient, durable, or permanent. Pound objects to gold as a single standard for money, because its material permanence ensures that "there is always more," in Derrida's phrase, than the value contained in less permanent goods. According to Pound, this supplementarity of gold leads to speculation in money for its own sake (usury), and "even the concept of energy being 'concentrated in money,' as if one were speaking of the divine quality of consecrated bread."[23]

The transformation that Pound protests, from money to bread to body, recalls the transformation from gold to "mother's milk" in "The Gift." In contrast to Pound, Williams is celebrating precisely "the energizing force of imagination," as he calls it in *Spring and All* (*CPI*: 220). But where usury hoards that energy, according to Pound, the imagination spends it, according to Williams. Thus, what Williams's economics represents as the gift, his physics represents as radioactivity, in which "something / is given off" (*CP1*: 219), a process that *Spring and All* links with that of "words freed by the imagination" (*CP1*: 234–35). Words, because it is a matter of the signifier: "The word must be put down for itself, not as a symbol of nature" (*CP1*: 189). But words thus put down do not become mere things, lying inertly on the page. They are the energy that is given off. Only in the form of energy does the materiality of the signifier interest Williams. He is not concerned with the lead left after radioactive decay, but with "Helium plus, plus / what? Never mind, but plus" (*P* 179). As for Derrida, for Williams the materiality of the signifier ensures that "there is always more." What would appear as mere by-product in some economies is in Williams's gift economy the very core of productivity.[24]

Williams's famous slogan "no ideas but in things" (*P* 6) is a formula for the sign—the signified is inseparable from the signifier—but it is commonly misread as a declaration of naive empiricism because Williams uses the word "things" where he means the materiality of the signifier, in the sense I have just outlined.[25] Similarly, Williams's frequent analogies between poetry and painting have proven to be misleading. By observing, for instance, that "[Gertrude] Stein has stressed, as Braque did paint, words" (*RI* 70), Williams has led critics to assume that he regards "words as things" that "can be put down on the page like splashes of paint on a canvas," as Hillis Miller has put it (*PR* 304). In fact, however, Williams is recognizing not merely the physical properties of paint but also the signifying properties of painting, at a basic level that Miller, for one, is unwilling to acknowledge. For Williams, once the analogy between words and paint has been established, words can be allowed to acquire meaning purely through what Williams calls "arrangement" (*RI* 70) or "design," "so that there would be a meaning without saying anything at all" (*Int* 53), as Williams discovered in the art of Cézanne.

The principle of design, "just the relation of the parts to themselves" (*Int* 53), encompasses what Saussure calls "difference," the value that words acquire solely by their place in a system of words.[26] But "difference" for Williams is also the "différance" that Derrida derives from his critique of Saussure. It is the excess of signification that enabled Brueghel to differ from his Italian masters, as Williams presents the London *Adoration* in "Pictures from Brueghel," where the excess is represented by "the brilliant / colors of the chronicler." As I noted in the preceding chapter, color is often regarded as the least definable element of painting, the element that continually escapes verbal formulation, just as the many paintings that Williams sets against his poems have frustrated critics by the very fact that they lie beyond the poems themselves. Williams regards color as "the same thing" as "the inarticulate design" (*RI* 233). That Brueghel's colors are said to be "of the chronicler" confirms color's relation to signification but does not limit the signifying function to mere recording.[27] Similarly, gold is made attractive to Williams not by any properties of "natural" representation, such as Pound would demand of it, but by its unnatural and coloristic qualities: "its indestructibility by air or acid, its malleability [having no "proper" shape, like Brueghel's Wise Men], its color and its sheen" (*RI* 162).

Within the medium of language, Williams recognizes such qualities in the activity of "playing the words" (*P* 179) that he associates with the discovery of radioactivity. It provides a touchstone of his criticism, for instance in his assessment of Góngora, who, in the same period as Brueghel, also found in the materiality of the signifier a means of escape from Italian classicism and a new form of wisdom: "he strained at the cords of the old meter, the old thoughts, refusing to adopt the Italianate modes of his immediate predecessors until the words broke like a bridge under him and he fell through among fragments— wisely" (*SE* 228). As I have tried to demonstrate in this chapter, Williams "fell" among fragments in his own poetry, where he also "played" such words as "proper," in the Brueghel passage in *Paterson* 5; or "knowledge," in his analysis of Shakespeare; or "mastery," as in the following stanza from the *Adoration* poem in "Pictures from Brueghel," here deliberately lifted from context to give a better idea of its material form:

> from the Italian masters
> but with a difference
> the mastery

Reading down the line breaks demonstrates that linguistic difference, as Derrida delights in pointing out, can be a matter of a single letter.[28] Between "masters" and "mastery," Williams accomplishes for Brueghel the same depersonalization that required many lines in Williams's prose analysis of Shakespeare in *Spring and All.*

It is "the mastery / of the painting," in the case of Brueghel, just as it is the power "of the imagination," in the case of Shakespeare, that Williams would celebrate. In removing the crown of mastery from the person of the artist, however, Williams does not elevate the crown to some transcendent realm, as if the imagination were Romantic Spirit. Rather, Williams's imagination inheres in "a language which we hear spoken about us every day" (*SL* 327). His Romantic inheritance is thus especially Wordsworthian, endowing the artist with a capability that can be measured in terms of ordinary experience. "That is what it is to be an artist with his material before him," writes Williams as a follow-up to his comparison of Stein and Braque. "It is to be a kind of laborer—a workman—a maker in a very plain sense—nothing vague or transcendental about it: that is the artist—at base" (*RI* 70–71).

That is the artist Williams sought to represent in the figure of Brueghel. In reading the "Self-Portrait" that Williams has set at the head of "Pictures from Brueghel" (*CP2*: 385), it is important not to confuse the traditional image of the artist as semidivine creator, inapplicable to this case, with that of "the painter as master of his craft," which does apply.[29] Lawson-Peebles falls into that confusion because for him, the craftsman is one who "exerts absolute control over his material," whereas for Williams, the craftsman has too much respect for his material to set himself above it. That is why so much of the "Self-Portrait" is given over to the depiction of "stuff"—"a heavy wool coat / with broad buttons"—and why such stuff blends with physiognomic detail normally read for spiritual significance: "a red winter hat blue / eyes smiling."[30]

This attitude toward material may be implicated in the relation of the northern artist Brueghel to the Italian tradition, a central issue in Williams's treatment of the London *Adoration* in "Pictures from Brueghel." Unlike the Italian painters' identification with "a literate elite," northerners, according to Svetlana Alpers, identified with "other craftsmen" (*AD* 112), as evident "in their concentration on rendering crafted stuffs" (*AD* 114). In lines that begin the transition from the Adoration passage in *Paterson* 5, Williams implies such a concentration in Brueghel: "the suits of his peasants were of better stuff, hand woven, than we can boast" (*P* 228). In contrast, modern insensitivity to material is represented in the protest of a Portuguese mason against "that stuff they sell you in the stores nowadays, no good, break in your hands," and in the protest of another voice, which seems more closely identified with Williams himself, against "this featureless tribe that has the money now—staring into the atom, completely blind."[31] The choice of the atom as the quintessentially modern material hints at the potentially destructive consequences of such blindness. We are reminded that, in Williams's study of Brueghel's *Adoration*, he discovered a blind incomprehension in the Soldiers.

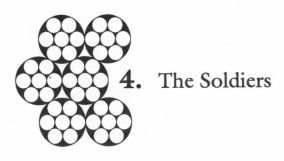

4. The Soldiers

THE TWO preceding chapters have demonstrated how Williams's exploration of the Epiphany scene involves questions about knowledge, both about its object, the thing known, and its agent, the one who is supposed to know.[1] In the introductory chapter, I suggested that such epistemological questions, although they appear primary in much recent critical theory, are in fact based on underlying ethical concerns. Knowledge has come under critique because it plays a role in establishing authority, and the exercise of authority is condemned, from an ethical perspective, as violence. Since violence has also traditionally been conceived as a means of opposing authority, however, the critique of authority may turn away from one sort of violence only to adopt another. Before exploring Williams's solution to this dilemma in subsequent chapters, I want to devote the present chapter to a full recognition of his involvement in it. In *Paterson* 3, Williams proclaims his "defiance of authority" in the context of a fire that destroys a library (*P* 119). In the Epiphany scene in *Paterson* 5, the potential for such violence, though it seems temporarily suspended, persists in the presence of the Soldiers.

Given their public function, we might expect the Soldiers to represent violence in the service of rather than in opposition to authority. That they function in both capacities simultaneously is evident from Williams's ambivalent attitude toward World War II, with which he associates Brueghel's Soldiers by comparing them with "the more stupid / German soldiers of the late / war." Because they are too stupid to comprehend the force they serve, that force has an equal chance of working for good or for ill, according to Williams. He recognized the Germans' hostile intentions in bombing London, for instance, but that violence had the beneficial result of clearing the city's slums, which Williams, prompted by the tales of his English grandmother, had long identified with a kind of institutional violence "that kills the senses."[2] As a political thesis, this argument seems remarkably insensitive to the human cost of such forced renewal, but Williams was seeking rather to argue an aesthetic thesis, to claim for the imagination the energies that were squandered in the stupidity of war. "The necessary destruction could have been better done, more economically, with less collateral waste through the agency of peace but only a violent peace dominated by revolution," Williams insisted in "Midas" (*RI* 167). It would be a peace such as "the revolutionary St. Francis" promised (*RI* 166), or such as Williams envisioned in "Burning the Christmas Greens" (1944), in which the "violence" of the fire produces in the imagination a pastoral scene, complementary to the arrangement of greens amid which Williams "put a herd of small / white deer" (*CP2*: 63). After burning the greens,

> we stood
> ourselves refreshed among
> the shining fauna of that fire.   (*CP2*: 65)

As if to separate for analysis the positive and negative aspects of the violence represented by Brueghel's Soldiers, Williams evokes that violence through two different sets of images. The first set, concerned with weapons, produces a strongly negative impression in the opening lines of the passage treating Brueghel's painting. Williams introduces the Soldiers as

> Armed men,
> savagely armed men
> armed with pikes,
> halberds and swords

This motif derives from traditional representations of the military guard who were assumed to have accompanied the three kings on their journey. In that role the Soldiers would perform a protective function. But the compressed verticality of Brueghel's composition, a highly unusual format for this artist, makes the Soldiers seem to oppress rather than protect the figures they loom above. As Rudolf Arnheim has remarked, "As soon as we notice the spear of the soldier striking the head of the Madonna, we realize that the threat of violence, the whispers of skepticism and gossip, the thrust of the armed multitude, are no mere accessories but essential to the painter's interpretation."[3]

The interpretation Arnheim seems to have in mind emerges more clearly in Brueghel's *The Massacre of the Innocents* (ca. 1565–67; fig. 8), where soldiers actively deploy their weapons against babies, in a scene that many commentators read as protest against political oppression in Brueghel's day.[4] Although Williams explicitly associates Brueghel's soldiers with Nazi troops, it seems likely that he also took them to represent a threat posed more universally to the promise represented by babies. "The birth of every baby, whatever its quality, is a revelation," Williams declared in a 1947 essay, but such "Revelation," as the essay is titled, faces a constant threat of extinction from the "adult guard" who seek to indoctrinate the baby in the forms of the past (*SE* 270). If the initial revelation is not thoroughly extinguished as the child matures, it will only be because the surrounding adults were "imperfectly armed," Williams noted sardonically.

The arms borne by the Soldiers in Brueghel's *Adoration* thus identify them as agents of oppression. In contrast, another attribute elicits more sympathy for the Soldiers as themselves the victims of oppression, and, if still the agents of violence, at least of a form of violence with which Williams could expect his readers to identify. Toward the end of his treatment of Brueghel's painting, Williams pictures the Soldiers with,

> ragged clothes,
> mouths open,
> their knees and feet
> broken from 30 years of
> war, hard campaigns, their mouths
> watering for the feast which
> had been provided[5]

Neither Brueghel's painting nor the biblical account of the Epiphany depicts a feast in the literal sense. Williams appears to have inferred its existence from the expression on the Soldiers' faces, where, however, eyes seem more noticeably open than mouths. The opinion of some commentators that the bespectacled man at the far right is staring with "hungry eyes" at the black king's gift suggests how Williams may have sensed the Soldiers' hunger.[6] I have already shown how Williams transforms the kings' gifts to "a mother's milk" in "The Gift"; what was there called "a child's / appetite" has been transferred to the Soldiers in *Paterson* 5. Or, rather, Williams seeks to draw our attention to a generally human appetite; there is nothing about the bespectacled man, for instance, to identify him specifically as a soldier. But, in both *Paterson* 5 and "Pictures from Brueghel," Williams designates the entire group of bystanders as "soldiers" in order to lend their appetite the connotations of violence.

This is a form of violence in which Williams himself is deeply implicated, and that he had long associated with Brueghel. Williams's earliest published reference to Brueghel appears, rather incongruously, in his study of the American experience, *In the American Grain*, written in 1924 while Williams and his wife enjoyed an extended European tour, the basis also for Williams's novel *A Voyage to Pagany*. During that tour, Williams visited the large collection of Brueghel paintings in the Kunsthistorisches Museum in Vienna, but the work that finds its way into *In the American Grain* is an early engraving, *Big Fish Eat Little Fish* (1557; fig. 9), which Williams studied in Paris with the bookseller and literary entrepreneur, Adrienne Monnier.[7] Williams reads Brueghel's print as an allegory of desire in the context of his sexual attraction to Monnier, whose conversation he reports with delight:

> To eat, to drink; wines, the delicious flesh, the poets—all good things of the world—these we must learn again to enjoy. Had she not wished to do with books, she would have enjoyed most to be a butcher, to kill a pig, to hear it squeal, eeeeEEEE! Bryher's eyes snapped darkly. We looked at prints of Brueghel; the great fish, cut open, discharging from its slit belly other fish and each fish, slit in turn, discharging other smaller fish, and so on to the smallest. She laughed with glee. Secretly my heart beat high. Here was invitation.[8]

Both Monnier's invitation and Williams's response to it are highly ambiguous. Williams introduces this scene with a confession: "could I have loosed myself to embrace this turning, shouting, rustling, colored thing, my mind would have been relieved. I could not do it." The force of European sensuality exposes to Williams the streak of American puritanism that resides within him, lending a special edge to his critique of that character in *In the American Grain*. Adding to his resistance, however, is his uncertainty whether the liberation to which Monnier seems to invite him might not prove to be a form of capture. The other woman involved in this scene, Winifred Ellerman (Bryher), had arranged a marriage with Williams's friend, Robert McAlmon, as a cover for her liaison with Hilda Doolittle (H. D.) (Mariani, *NWN* 177–79). We begin to see the fish lining up in order of their size, each waiting to swallow the other, and Williams is by no means sure he is the largest. "Adrienne gave no quarter to any man," Williams observed in his *Autobiography*. "Once, when Bob [McAlmon] in a taxi had taken her in his arms and kissed her, she sunk her teeth into his lips so that he expected to have a piece torn out before she released him" (*A* 193).

After his return to America, Williams shared his impressions of Monnier with Sylvia Beach, another woman whose attraction to Monnier Williams had noted. "She has left me with a picture of French women carrying the men in their hair," Williams wrote to Beach (Mariani, *NWN* 245). Nevertheless, despite, or perhaps because, of its threatening tone, Williams vowed he would never forget the squeal Monnier made in imitation of a pig being slaughtered. He still remembered it when he wrote his first poem on Brueghel, "The Dance" (1944), after *The Kermess* (ca. 1567; fig. 2) at Vienna.[9] Not only "the squeal and the blare and the / tweedle of bagpipes" to which the peasants dance, but also the soundness of the "shanks" they dance on, recalls the earthiness of the "heavy-legged" Monnier (*A* 222).

The triangulation of Williams, Monnier, and Brueghel is worth dwelling on for the insights it offers into the violence that Williams associates with Brueghel's Soldiers. It leads, for instance, beyond the kings' gifts and locates the ultimate object of the Soldiers' desire in the Virgin, the visual terminus of one soldier's spear, as Arnheim notes. I have suggested that Williams credits the Soldiers' gaze with a similarly aggressive force.[10] Having acknowledged the symbolic implications of the spear, I would designate its force as phallic, though Williams makes that association more explicitly in the case of the gaze. *Paterson* 2 develops the phallic properties of the observation tower that "stands up prominently / from its pubic grove" (*P* 53), and much earlier, in the poem "March" (1916), a gaze associated with that of a snake carries the power to impregnate.

"March" is Williams's first poem to declare its occasion in a specific work of visual art, in this case an Annunciation by Fra Angelico.[11] In a chilling image, Williams depicts,

> the angel's eyes
> holding the eyes of Mary
> as a snake's hold a bird's.   (*CP1*: 140)

How much of the chill is to be credited to Williams, rather than Angelico, can be gauged by observing, first, that Williams has chosen to construct a simile rather than merely describe the painting, and second, that the circumstance on which the simile is based is Williams's invention, since in the painting Mary's gaze does not meet that of the angel. The sense of violence that Williams attributes to their encounter is reinforced by the context in which he sets it. For instance, in lines based on an Assyrian bas-relief, Williams depicts arrows bristling from the backs of wounded lions.[12] And a passage that Williams eventually canceled had announced "flowers / thronging / thicker than the Germans through Brussels!" (*CP1*: 494).

Recalling Williams's imagery of Germans in World War II will help in reading this image of the Germans in World War I as another example of the renovating power that Williams attributed to violence, comparable to the forces of March that set spring flowers marching. But in the poem "March" the sense of violence overwhelms the sense of renovation, perhaps because Williams was trying to embrace the violence directly, which he found he could not do in his encounter with Adrienne Monnier. Brueghel served Williams in that encounter in very much the way that he served a number of writers, including Williams, in their effort to approach the enormity of World War II without being overwhelmed.[13] Violence is present in Brueghel's work, but it is typically displaced from the point at which the viewer is invited to take up his or her position, as the Soldiers in the London *Adoration* are displaced, for instance, or the drowning boy in the famous *Landscape with the Fall of Icarus* (fig. 12). *Big Fish Eat Little Fish* is the most openly violent work by Brueghel to which Williams refers, but even in that case the viewer, identified perhaps with the father who explains the scene to his son at the lower left, relates to violence through cool analysis, or at most, active dissection.

In the American Grain provides an occasion for Williams's analysis of the desire at work within him in relation to a distinction between two types of violence, a European type that is the expression of desire and an American type that is an attempt to escape desire. "We believe that life in America is compact of violence and the shock of immediacy. This is not so," Williams observes.[14] Rather, "the characteristic of American life is that it holds off from embraces, from impacts, gaining, by fear, safety and time in which to fortify its prolific carcass— while the spirit, with tongue hanging out, bites at its bars—its object just out of reach" (*IAG* 175).

This is the condition that Williams depicts in the poem from *Spring and All* separately titled "To Elsie," where violence is abundant but "without / emotion" (*CP1*: 217), because it functions to separate rather than join spirit and body:

> as if the earth under our feet
> were
> an excrement of some sky
>
> and we degraded prisoners
> destined
> to hunger until we eat filth
>
> while the imagination strains
> after deer
> going by fields of goldenrod in
>
> the stifling heat of September   (*CP1*: 218)

The plight of Brueghel's Soldiers, as Williams understands it, is recognizable here in Williams's description of "prisoners / destined / to hunger." But another sort of hunger is evident in the imagination's straining after deer. In contrast to "Burning the Christmas Greens," this pastoral scene is "stifling" rather than refreshing because the imagination suffers just as much as desire when the two forces are isolated from each other.

Both sides of this isolation are again apparent in Williams's presentation of the "Beautiful Thing" in *Paterson* 3. Like Elsie in *Spring and All*, the woman whom Williams calls "Beautiful Thing" has suffered physical abuse. Williams, or his persona, "Dr. Paterson," is called in to attend to her as a physician, but his desire propels him toward her as a lover. However, unlike "the guys from Paterson" (*P* 127), who broke the woman's nose, the doctor channels his desire away from the body. As he pictures the woman with the "dazzled half sleepy eyes / . . . of some trusting animal" (*P* 109), we can feel him straining after the deer of some impossible pastoral. Surely, it is no earthly animal that "makes a temple / of its place of savage slaughter" (*P* 109), as Williams says the Beautiful Thing has done.

Of all of Williams's lines on the Beautiful Thing, these, in my view, best support Sandra Gilbert's and Susan Gubar's charge that Williams "formulates a worshipful philosophy about her suffering."[15] The charge is an especially serious one in the context of this study, for Williams claims that Brueghel painted the Virgin "as a work of art / for profound worship," and Gilbert and Gubar imply that such treatment commits a kind of violence that is comparable to, though not identical with, the violence that gave the Beautiful Thing her broken nose. I have already posited a similar complementary relationship between the brutality of desire and the straining of imagination, both symptoms of the peculiarly "twisted" condition of desire in the American character as Williams analyzes it (*IAG* 178).

To carry out this analysis, however, Williams must have found some way of working through that character as it was manifested in himself. This is what he is about, I believe, in the passage that Gilbert and Gubar cite as the primary evidence in their case against Williams:

> I must believe that all
> desired women have had each
>> in the end
>> a busted nose
> and live afterward marked up
>> Beautiful Thing
>> for memory's sake
> to be credible in their deeds   (*P* 127)

Rather than making a temple of a place of slaughter, this passage seems designed to keep the slaughter exposed "for memory's sake," just as Williams swore never to forget Adrienne Monnier's squeal in imitation of a slaughtered pig. The sensuality that so astonished Williams in Monnier is also the quality that fascinates him in the Beautiful Thing, and her broken nose is a part of that fascination. However, to describe the fascination as "voyeuristic," as Gilbert and Gubar employ that term, is to overemphasize Williams's detachment from the experience, his need for "the guys from Paterson" to perform an action that he cannot bring himself to perform, or even his need for the Beautiful Thing to suffer a pain that he cannot bring himself to suffer.[16] In the view of Gilbert and Gubar, Williams exhibits "an oddly neo–Swinburnean pleasure in his own difference from, and superiority to, what he sees as ontological pain."[17]

I would agree that such difference is part of Williams's experience, but the joy of that experience, I would argue, derives from the dissolution of difference, as Williams immerses himself in the violence that surrounds and informs the figure of the Beautiful Thing. Just as he exulted in the clearing of British slums by German bombs, Williams exulted in the violence of desire because it undermined the temples he kept building in his imagination. Temples could be structures of oppression as much as slums, Williams knew.[18] "Their time past, / relief!" he exclaims as he commits the Christmas greens to the fire (*CP2*: 63). And just as he feels "refreshed" by a vision of peace within that fire, Williams is touched by the "quietness" that he perceives at the heart of the Beautiful Thing (*P* 104, 125). "It is," he concludes in *Paterson* 3, "a sort of chant, a sort of praise, a / peace that comes of destruction" (*P* 132).

Like Adrienne Monnier, the Beautiful Thing fascinates Williams as an agent of destruction. Although she enters the story of *Paterson* 3 as a victim, in the poem's symbolic network she is identified as a source of violence, allied with the force of fire:

> Whirling flames, leaping
>   from house to house, building to building
>
>   carried by the wind
>
>   the Library is in their path
>
>   Beautiful thing! aflame   .
>
>   a defiance of authority   (*P* 118–19)

If the fire defies the authority of the past enshrined in the Library, the Beautiful Thing defies the authority of the present enshrined in the person of Dr. Paterson. "Shaken" by her beauty (*P* 125), for "beauty is / a defiance of authority" (*P* 119), he cannot maintain his professional composure. When he asks her to remove her clothes, he feels desire rather than medical knowledge to be his motive. He speaks "in a fury, for which I am / ashamed" (*P* 105). This scene strikingly recalls Williams's short story "The Use of Force" (1933), in which the medical examination of a young girl takes on, in the doctor's own account, all the features of a rape. As the girl resists examination—in this case she is asked to open her mouth rather than remove her clothes—the doctor responds with "a blind fury, a feeling of adult shame, bred of a longing for muscular release" (*FD* 135).

Both the poem and the story are remarkable not only for the force of the emotions they reveal but also for the analysis of the emotions that Williams appears to undertake simultaneously with the experience. Williams's "shame" betokens a judgment passed on his "fury," as *Paterson* 3 makes clear, but "The Use of Force" reveals, further, that the shame is "bred of a longing for muscular release." We must not, then, identify the fury with the longing. The latter is the force of desire that Williams felt Adrienne Monnier inviting him to express. "My mind would have been relieved," he tells us, but "I could not do it" (*IAG* 106). Thus made aware of what he could not do, Williams came to a new understanding of the feeling consequent on that failure, a "fury" that results from the repression of desire in the American character. "Why then all this fury, this multiplicity we push between ourselves and our desires?" he asks in a later chapter of *In the American Grain* (*IAG* 178). His answer: "It is bred of fear" (*IAG* 175).

Williams's further analysis of that fear in *In the American Grain* was influenced by his trip to Vienna, where he deepened his acquaintance not only with Brueghel but also with Freud. His reading of Freud's *Beyond the Pleasure Principle*, which he found in a Viennese bookstore, provided a theoretical framework for the distinction he was developing between the European and the American relation to desire. In his fictionalized account of his European tour, *A Voyage to Pagany* (1928), Williams's persona, Dev Evans, decides that Paris has its American side, "its frivolity, its frantic milling about for pleasure," but in its heart, Paris is "*Jenseits des Lust-prinzips*"—the German title of Freud's book.[19] In *In the American Grain*, Williams elaborates: "There is a kind of piling of experience upon experience that is not bound to satiety, but to wisdom, the highest knowledge of all, to Buddha, if one likes, to release, to relief, to the dangerous ground of pleasure: *Jenseits des lust princip* [*sic*], Freud sees it, beyond the charmed circle," that is, the circle of pleasure (*IAG* 176). "It is no matter," Williams continues, "since it is unknown in the province I am discussing," that is, in America, where "through terror, there is no direct touch." The "fury" that Williams detects in the American character, then, is the fear of touch, most immediately. Ultimately, it is fear of "the dangerous ground of pleasure."

By distinguishing pleasure from another kind of experience, "dangerous" yet still related to pleasure, as its "ground," Williams anticipated more recent French theorists who call the latter experience *jouissance*, a "joy ripped with pain," in the concise formulation of Julia Kristeva (*DL* 184). A series of correspondences between Williams and Kristeva, which I will pursue further in later chapters, may be said to arise from their understanding of jouissance. Located "beyond the pleasure principle," and tied to the death instinct that Freud postulated in that realm "beyond," jouissance manifests death mainly as a shattering of the sense of self.[20] The experience is in some ways analogous to the deconstruction of the knowing subject that I examined in the preceding chapter, but while deconstructive critics make the shat-

THE SOLDIERS • 55

tering appear to be the whole point of the experience, psychoanalytic critics such as Kristeva, who are more inclined to use the term "jouissance," tend to assign it a role in the process by which the subject is constituted, however provisionally (*PH* 9–10).

In Kristeva's application of this theory, modern literature involves the reader in a continual cycle of deconstitution and reconstitution. "Our only chance to avoid being neither master nor slave of meaning," she writes, "lies in our ability to insure our mastery of it (through technique or knowledge) as well as our passage through it (through play or practice). In a word, jouissance" (*DL* x). Williams suspends *Paterson* 3 between similar poles, calling "for relief from 'meaning' " in the first section (*P* 111) and finding it in the destructive forces of fire and water that course throughout the book, but concluding with an equally forceful commitment:

> I must
> find my meaning and lay it, white,
> beside the sliding water   (*P* 145)

In the following chapters, I will examine the interaction between construction and destruction in Williams's treatment of Brueghel's Epiphany. For the present chapter, the focus will remain on destruction, now seen, however, through the psychoanalytic lens that Williams began to fashion through his reading of Freud.

According to the notion of jouissance elaborated by Kristeva, the "dangerous ground" on which Williams locates that experience would be the body of the mother, rendered fearful to touch under the terms of the incest taboo (*PH* 6, 63–64). Williams dallies with the notion of incest through the relation of Dev Evans and his sister in *A Voyage to Pagany*, but the mother herself looms up in *In the American Grain* as the ground of the New World, a precise equivalent to what Julia Kristeva calls "the maternal continent" (*KR* 318). Anticipating "The Delineaments of the Giants," with which he would open *Paterson* (6), Williams begins a portrayal of the New World as an "elemental giant" (*IAG* 10), in the chapter of *In the American Grain* treating the voyages of Columbus: "The New World, existing in those times beyond the sphere of all things known to history, lay in the fifteenth century as the middle of the desert or the sea lies now and must lie forever, marked with its own dark life which goes on to an immaculate fulfillment in which we have no part" (*IAG* 7).

Columbus takes his place in Williams's study as the first of many examples of men's inability, on the one hand, to tolerate that in which they have no part, and on the other hand, to conceive of themselves as a part of another being.[21] From "Columbus' infatuated course" (7) to Raleigh's ill-fated efforts at "plunging his lust into the body of a new world" (59), Williams poses the dilemma in terms of sexual desire. As the word "immaculate" already hints in the statement on Columbus quoted above, the object of desire is a virgin, "ravished" by the fury of men's lust (7). In 1921, Williams had identified that lust as his own, in a thinly fictionalized account of his adventures with the Baroness Elsa von Freytag-Loringhoven: "America, since his boyhood, had stood before the heated imagination of Evan Dionysius Evans as a virginal young woman—inclined, of course, to grant important favors to certain individuals of special distinction."[22]

The identification of the Virgin with the New World complicates but does not contradict Williams's handling of the Epiphany scene, where the Baby, as I have argued, brings the revelation that Williams associates with the New World. In a later chapter of *In the American Grain*, the voice that speaks for the continent, designated as "She," identifies herself with her "son," the Indian chief Tuscaloosa (*IAG* 48). As my later chapters will show, Virgin and Baby become increasingly difficult to distinguish in the Epiphany scene as well. The fusion of mother and son is, after all, the dream of incest. Their separation, in opposition to incest, can be understood to be the goal of that violence that Williams explores in the American character. In Kristeva's terms, it is "the immemorial violence with which a body becomes separated from another body in order to be," and for which her name is "abjection" (*PH* 10). The fragile self situated on this frontier of being is subject to the fear of being devoured, reabsorbed, by the other from which it is barely separated (*PH* 62). One defense is to devour the other first but then to throw out, or abject, what has been devoured, in a continual renewal of separation "in order to be" (cf. *PH* 53–54).

According to this scenario, the Soldiers who threaten the Virgin with violence are responding to her threat to them. Williams shows them gathering, in just this spirit, in the chapter that immediately follows Columbus's encounter with the Virgin in *In the American Grain*: "Upon the orchidean beauty of the new world the old rushed inevitably to revenge itself after the Italian's return" (*IAG* 27). The object of their revenge is exposed at the heart of Aztec culture, eventually destroyed by the soldiers of Cortez. The mixture of horror and fascination in Williams's account of the Aztec religion anticipates the mood in which he records his response to Adrienne Monnier several chapters later. The blood of slaughter, human sacrifice in the case of the Aztecs, features prominently in both accounts, as does the violence of hunger, linked in both cases to a fear of women. Commenting on "the instinctive exclusion of women from all places of worship; the debarring of priests from female society" in the Aztec religion, Williams explains, "it was a ceremonial acknowledgment of the deep sexless urge of life itself, the hungry animal, underlying all other power" (*IAG* 34). Kristeva devotes a third of her study of abjection, *The Powers of Horror*, to an analysis of such exclusion in religious practices. Her analysis suggests that the "urge" these practices acknowledge, through a fanatical insistence on sexual difference, is "sexless" insofar as it threatens to erase sexual difference along with the primal separation of subject and object. The sexlessness of the Virgin poses a similar threat, which religious practice has similarly sought to control (*PH* 64; cf. *TL* 235–37). It is no accident that Cortez replaces the Aztec idols with "images of Our Lady and the saints" (*IAG* 34).

To explain the threat posed to the male psyche by the female sex, psychoanalysis has traditionally invoked the fear of castration. Women can arouse that fear by appearing to have been castrated. They can also, however, appear as the agents of castration through an aggressive orality such as Williams attributes to Brueghel's Soldiers.[23] In the larger context of Williams's images of women, their aggression equals that of the Soldiers, and it is difficult to say which came first. We might describe Robert McAlmon's attempt to kiss Adrienne Monnier as an act of aggression, for instance, but the aggressiveness was brought out more clearly when Monnier "sunk her teeth into his lips so that he expected to have a piece torn out," and no psychoanalyst would understand that piece to be merely of the lips. Similarly, the mere fact of the doctor's visit might have seemed aggressive to the young girl in "The Use of Force," but the doctor feels her aggression before he even proposes to examine her, and it thus seems to him to be unprovoked. From the very first, "the child was fairly eating me up with her cold, steady eyes" (*FD* 131). The ensuing battle between patient and doctor unfolds as a battle over the eyes, whose loss Freud took to symbolize castration.[24] When the doctor proposes to "take a look" at his patient's throat, she pokes at his eyes "instinctively" (*FD* 132) and succeeds in knocking his glasses off, but the doctor persists in his "blind fury," and in the end, "tears of defeat blinded her eyes" (*FD* 135).

If both doctor and patient experience a form of blindness at the end of "The Use of Force," both are initially endowed with a potency that psychoanalysis would identify as phallic. The female who threatens castration in Williams's work, even if she is only a young girl, represents that shadowy figure that Freud occasionally referred to as the "phallic mother," a product of that period in a child's development when the mother is still the primary point of orientation but the phallus has become the primary emblem of value, or even of being. At this stage, the child has not fully taken into account the anatomical differences between the sexes, nor even the distinction between mother and father.[25]

The resulting ambiguity seems to persist in Williams's tendency to vacillate between male and female images when he seeks to represent the power toward which he oriented both his life and his art. On the one hand, for example, he credits his career as a poet to his being "early inducted into my father's habit of reading," but on the other hand, he admits that it would have given him "at least as great a satisfaction" to have become a painter like his mother.[26] Even the art of writing seems to derive from the mother when Williams claims that "to progress from word to word is to suck a nipple" (*I* 159), but the object of such orality may be male as well as female. The imagination that furnishes "a mother's milk" in "The Gift" and justifies "a view of the mind / that, in a way, gives milk" in "May 1st Tomorrow" (1949; *CP2*: 189) also informs the more traditional and more patriarchal imagery of "The Host" (1953):

> There is nothing to eat,
>> seek it where you will,
>>> but of the body of the Lord.   (*CP2*: 260)

A remarkable passage in the manuscript of Williams's "Midas" essay shows a similar ambivalence in his use of phallic imagery. To oppose the destructive forces unleashed in World War II, Williams proposes "a flagrant disclosure" (*RI* 169), apparently like that of the young lovers, "flagrant in desire" (*P* 71), whom Paterson observes in the park in *Paterson* 2. In "Midas," Williams envisions "some Rabelaisian monumentation: an ingot of gold such as might be made of the metal in the vaults of Kentucky—a golden bar fifty feet long, twenty-five feet wide and twenty high." Once he has raised such a monument, however, Williams cannot decide what to do with it, and his indecision takes the form of vacillation between male and female images. On the male side, the ingot might be "molded upon a gigantic death mask of J. P. Morgan," then set up in Death Valley, where "it would be visited and gaped at by millions," an appropriately phallic tribute to the phallus, in light of the power ascribed to the gaze in "March" or "The Use of Force." On the female side in "Midas," the phallic gaze is eluded, and the presiding deity, unlike the patriarch Morgan, remains anonymous, but we should have no difficulty in recognizing the mother when the monument is "molten in a gigantic pot and poured into the sea." The sea and the desert, the two places to which Williams consigns the phallus in "Midas," are the two places that he invokes in *In the American Grain* as modern equivalents of the New World in the time of Columbus (*IAG* 7). All are images of the mother in her "immaculate fulfillment in which we have no part."

The gesture of committing the phallus to the sea accomplishes both fulfillment and destruction, coition and castration. Williams expounds the combination most fully in the chapter in *In the American Grain* on Hernando de Soto, whose discovery of the Mississippi River appears as a sexual conquest. "Now you are over, you have straddled me, this is my middle," concedes the voice of the New World. But "I am not defeated," "She" warns (*IAG* 52). "Still there is that which you have not sounded, under the boats, under the adventure—giving to all things the current, the wave, the onwash of my passion" (*IAG* 53). De Soto does not sound these depths until, after suffering much hardship, including a suggestive wound in the thigh (*IAG* 49), he dies and is buried in the Mississippi: "Down, down, this solitary sperm, down into the liquid, the formless, the insatiable belly of sleep" (*IAG* 58). Sperm, phallus, and body as a whole, de Soto is wholly devoured by that insatiable belly.

In *Paterson*, Williams explores another river, New Jersey's Passaic, whose course also follows the current of desire.[27] Toward the conclusion of book 4, where Williams at one time thought to end his poem, the river reaches the sea, an "immaculate" mother, like the New World discovered by Columbus but now steeped in the past:[28]

> Thalassa
> immaculata: our home, our nostalgic
> mother in whom the dead, enwombed again
> cry out to us to return .   (*P* 202)

Earlier, the same cry, "O Thalassa, Thalassa! / the lash and hiss of water," is heard in *Paterson* 3 (*P* 101), where it also emanates from the dead, calling from the books in the library: "Dead men's dreams, confined by these walls, risen, / seek an outlet" (*P* 100). The seductive force of their call is comparable to the attraction of the Beautiful Thing, but to submit to either, Williams warns, is to run the risk of castration:

> Beautiful Thing!
>
> —the cost of dreams
> in which we search, after a surgery
> of the wits and must translate, quickly
> step by step or be destroyed—under a spell
> to remain a castrate   (*P* 101)

A similar risk is implied at the end of *Paterson* 4 in the image of the sea spread with seed, evidently the product of Uranus's castration by his son Cronus. Out of that seed, as in the myth, rises the goddess of love, Aphrodite. Williams calls her Venus, in recollection of Botticelli's famous painting of *The Birth of Venus* (ca. 1480), depicting "a girl standing upon a tilted shell, rose /pink."[29]

Despite the attractiveness of this image, it threatens something fundamental in Williams's make-up, something even more fundamental than the value of the phallus that is threatened by the prospect of castration. Before *Paterson* 4 concludes, it undergoes a dramatic shift of register from a mythic to a realistic mode. Instead of a girl, or a goddess, a man emerges from the sea, where he has been swimming. After picking some beach plums and "spitting the seed out," he heads inland, in a gesture that seems to confirm the earlier objection, "the sea is *not* our home" (*P* 203, 201). Williams's first comments on this conclusion corroborate Kristeva's observation that the subject in abjection faces "the loss not of a part (castration) but of the totality of his living being . . . of his very own identity," by "sinking irretrievably into the mother" (*PH* 64). The sea in *Paterson* marks the place "where the river appears to have lost its identity," Williams explained.[30] He wrote to Marianne Moore in a more personal vein: "If I did not achieve a language I at least stated what I would not say. I would not melt myself into the great universal sea (of love) with all its shapes and colors" (*SL* 304). It is no accident, then, that the goddess of love appears at the end of *Paterson* 4 as she is represented in a painting, "with all its shapes and colors." Painting was well suited to exploit the seductiveness of matter that Williams both loved and feared. "Liquid" and "formless," as modern artists were revealing with ever–increasing emphasis, painting seemed to open on that "insatiable belly" that swallowed Hernando de Soto.

The horror of such a fate, clearly registered whenever Williams contemplates it, has misled many critics to the conclusion that Williams attempts to escape it. Paul Bové's commentary on the end of *Paterson*

4 may be taken as representative in this regard, and its peculiarly Heideggerian perspective is additionally useful for the prominence it assigns to themes that are central to this study: "The poet not only refuses the movement back to an 'origin,' the sea and its wrecks, but rejects as well the Sirenic attractions of yielding consciousness and subjectivity, that is, authority, to an already 'present' death disguised as the great Mother. The poet must not surrender entirely to matter."[31] Against such a reading, I would argue that Williams is continually yielding authority even as he asserts it, in the double process articulated in Julia Kristeva's statement on jouissance quoted earlier. Witnessing violence in another, the observer experiences that violence in himself, at the same time that he retains a position of detachment from the experience. This process is at work in the relationship between Williams and Adrienne Monnier, "Dr. Paterson" and the Beautiful Thing, and the doctor and his young patient in "The Use of Force." It is also at work in the conclusion of *Paterson* 4.

Statements such as Bové's construe that conclusion as if Williams's persona came to the edge of the sea, contemplated its terrors, and then turned away. But Williams introduces the man as a swimmer, emerging from the sea, in which he has immersed himself so completely that at first he cannot be identified as a man:

> What's that?
> —a duck, a hell-diver? A swimming dog?
> What, a sea-dog? There it is again.
> A porpoise, of course, following
> the mackerel   . —No. Must be the up-
> end of something sunk. But this is moving!
> Maybe not. Flotsam of some sort.   (*P* 202)

Here is the loss of identity that Williams associated with the sea. It is recorded from a position on shore, such as Bové imagines, but detachment from the sea should not be misunderstood as rejection of it. Through the operation of his language, the observer participates in the swimmer's experience; loss of identity is felt as loss of the ability to identify. At the same time, some measure of control over that loss is permitted by its translation into language, or, let us say, into signifying process, in order not to exclude the "language" of painting, which Williams introduces by way of Botticelli. If Williams does not "submit entirely to matter," as Bové argues, it is because the matter that attracts him is the materiality of the signifier. Rather than culminating in a final loss of identity, a signifying process that remains open to materiality moves, as Kristeva likes to put it, "from one identity to another."[32]

The emergence of the swimmer from the sea at the end of *Paterson* 4 is a part of that movement. Although he turns inland, the swimmer does not put the sea, with its joys and terrors, irrevocably behind him, for ahead of him lies "a distant / waterfall," far upstream at Paterson, whose sound is recalled in the "steady roar" of the sea (*P* 203), and whose violent fall is brutally figured in the book's final image, that of a public hanging. But the swimmer's emergence from formless fluidity into identifiable form indicates that the passage through violence may lead to a new mode of existence, sufficiently different to tempt Williams to call it peace. If the violence explored in this chapter arises through separation, as Kristeva's psychoanalytic model suggests, the peace that emerges from that violence heals separation through identification. After exploring separation in *Powers of Horror*, Kristeva went on to explore identification in *Tales of Love*. Williams progressed through a similar sequence as he reopened *Paterson* and set out to write a fifth book.[33]

"*Paterson* V must be written, is being written," Williams told an interviewer in 1957. "Why must it be written?" he asked. Because "*Paterson* IV ends with the protagonist breaking through the bushes, identifying himself with the land, with America" (*IWWP* 22). The image of "breaking through the bushes" speaks for the urge, always present in Williams, to assert mastery, to take possession. But the reference to identification suggests a different urge from that which drove the various conquerors whom Williams chronicles in *In the American Grain*. "If the land were to be possessed," Williams writes in that book, "it must be as the Indian possessed it. . . . as a natural part of a beloved condition, the New World, in which all lived together" (*IAG* 137, 138). "There must be a new wedding," Williams declares (*IAG* 137). He celebrates it in *Paterson* 5 as the marriage of Mary and Joseph.

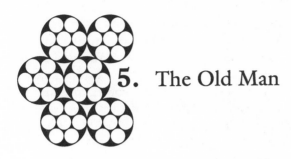

5. The Old Man

WILLIAMS'S own marriage features prominently in the writing that leads from the completion of *Paterson* 4 to the beginning of *Paterson* 5. The poem he thought was that beginning turned into "Asphodel," Williams's love poem to his wife, which concludes with the declaration,

>   It is late
>   but an odor
>   as from our wedding
>   has revived for me
>   and begun again to penetrate
>   into all crevices
>   of my world.   (*CP2*: 337)

"Asphodel" had begun just as Williams completed *The Build-Up* (Mariani, *NWN* 645), the third novel in his trilogy about his wife's family, leading up to the time when Flossie, as Williams called his wife, agrees to marry Charlie Bishop, the young doctor who is Williams's persona. As Charlie proposes marriage, he imagines, "it would be a marriage that would be founded on human understanding that would be difficult but passionate, passionate as one says of a saint—those saints that were womanly, or, like St. Francis, full of compassion" (*BU* 262–63).

The saint we are given in *Paterson* 5, however, is St. Joseph, whose story, particularly as it is presented through Brueghel's *Adoration*, contains a major obstacle to the construction of an ideal image of marriage. In the century before Brueghel, painters had begun to grant Joseph greater prominence in scenes from the life of Christ as part of a general tendency, encouraged by Franciscan teaching, toward humanizing that story. The question of humanity inevitably involved the question of sexuality. Brueghel's London *Adoration* appears to be unique, however, in presenting the question of sexuality as "straight-forward gossip," in the form of the words being whispered into Joseph's ear.[1] Most art historians, like most critics of Williams, assume those words taunt Joseph by doubting that he could be the father of the Baby whom Mary holds on her lap. In the context of *Paterson*, that suspicion seems to confirm a pattern that Robert Lowell noticed as early as the publication of the second book (1948): "everything strains toward marriage, but the marriages never come off, except in the imagination, and there, attenuated, fragmentary, and uncertain."[2]

We may be tempted to accept such a view as readily as we accept the chronicle of failed marriages that Lowell recorded in his own poetry, but Williams's poetry aims to prevent the ready acceptance of any form of conventional wisdom. The motif of the cuckolded husband is of course an ancient convention. A more modern one is the disbelief in the traditional religious account of the birth of Mary's Baby. Paul Mariani combines these two conventions to explain why Joseph, in Brueghel's painting, appears willing to tolerate the doubt cast on his status as the Baby's father. Naive enough to let his wife betray him in the first place, Joseph is also naive enough to accept her explanation when the evidence of that betrayal stares him in the face. Mary is "able to convince poor Joseph that her pregnancy had been the work of the Spirit" (*NWN* 9). Like most critics who have considered the issue, Mariani fails to consider the one possibility that best preserves the tensions that sustain the Brueghel passage in *Paterson* 5: Joseph recognizes the Baby as evidence of Mary's involvement with a lover, but he does not view that involvement as necessarily fatal to the marriage.

The best evidence for this interpretation lies within *Paterson*, but another text, Williams's "Prose About Love," offers supporting evidence of Williams's intention. Published in 1918, less than six years after Williams's marriage to Florence Herman, "Prose About Love" reveals a philosophical attitude toward marriage that is accurately reconstructed in the account of the proposal in *The Build-Up*. One surmises that Williams's attitude in fact did not change significantly over the years.[3] "For lovers to deride the husband as one who has been fooled," Williams warns in "Prose About Love," "is not only bad taste but may be as often as not inaccurate observation."[4] On the other hand, the husband's equanimity depends on "the accuracy with which his own life has been conceived," including his philosophy of marriage. According to Williams's philosophy, "the heart has springtimes every year. So it has its winters and so a man should separate from his wife at the time of some foreign love longing on either part." In Brueghel's painting, Williams would have found such separation visibly depicted in the way Joseph leans back from the semicircle formed by the main actors in the scene. But he does not leave that semicircle altogether. In "Prose About Love," Williams emphasizes, "separation removes the necessity for idle pretenses but by no means alters the conjugal attachment of husband and wife." A central thesis of this chapter, and indeed of this book, is that separation, as Williams eventually conceived it, constitutes a form of attachment in the relations of husband and wife, but also of poem and painting, reader and text. In each case, the attachment will go unnoticed unless we can conceive of a relation that is not a form of possession.

Both in contemporary theories of reading and in practical criticism, it is assumed that in relation to the text, the reader will be figured as "both possessing it and possessed by it."[5] In *Spring and All*, on the other hand, along with "the classic caress of author and reader," Williams also offers the image of "a fraternal embrace" (*CP1*: 178), as if he sought to resist the implications of the "classic" image. As an alternative, fraternity implies a relationship that combines intimacy and distance, equality and difference. Though it presumes partners of the same sex, it would be an error to conclude that the tensions of the fraternal relation, as conceived by Williams, are somehow sexless. All tension, in Williams's view, is fundamentally sexual. Accordingly, "sex is at the bottom of all art," he declares, because art seeks "to accomplish simultaneity," for which "we must have had two, multiplicity, the male and the female, man and woman—acting together, the fecundating principle" (*A* 373). As a number of critics have demonstrated, Williams's application of the principle of simultaneity in his poetry owes much to modernist experimentation in the visual arts.[6] His interest in those arts cannot be separated from his "fraternal" relation with his brother, Edgar. As the two set out on their separate careers, the aspiring poet wrote to the aspiring architect, "if you can influence the best that is in me by your architecture which you can do and if I can influence the best that is in you by expressing what I feel there could not possibly be any more joyful outlet to our love."[7]

Williams imagines a similar love between Joseph and Mary, but because he sets that love in the context of conventional expectations, it may seem to fall short of a "joyful outlet." The phrase "poor Joseph," employed by Mariani as he reads a narrative of marital infidelity into the Epiphany scene (*NWN* 9, 708), reflects Williams's language, but not his attitude. The language appears in a passage in *Paterson* 4 that anticipates the fuller treatment of Joseph in book 5. The context in book 4 is the story of another Mary, Marie Curie, whom Williams portrays as being "pregnant" with the discovery of radium (*P* 176). Like Joseph, Curie's husband, Pierre, is challenged by a wife whose "pregnancy" will produce a result that he will have no right to claim as his own. Nevertheless, again like Joseph, "Curie, the man, gave up / his work to buttress her."[8] This is the point at which Williams supplies the phrase that Mariani picks up:

> Poor Joseph,

the Italians say.

Glory to God in the highest
and on earth, peace, goodwill to
men!

Believe it or not.   (*P* 176)

Belief is the issue, as Mariani recognizes. But this passage lends no support to Mariani's assumption that, along with the "Italians" to whom Williams alludes, Williams himself is laughing at Joseph's capacity for belief. Rather, Williams is testing our capacity for belief by a method he employs throughout *Paterson*. He juxtaposes two texts offering opposed viewpoints, in this case the skeptical Italian joke and the biblical statement of faith, neither of which carries the authority of Williams's authorship. He then leaves it to us to decide between them. The formula, "Believe it or not," reenacts the gesture with which, in *Paterson* 3, Williams offers his own words to his readers: "The poem moves them or / it does not move them" (*P* 100).

As Williams's readers, we are in the position of Joseph. We can refuse to participate in the fiction presented to us, about whose status as fiction Williams permits no illusions: "I have told you, this / is a fiction" (*P* 236). But if we refuse, a very real achievement may be aborted, something as real to the liberated modern mind as the advance in scientific knowledge accomplished by Marie Curie. As Williams presents it, her accomplishment begins in the same act of the mind that her husband performs when he puts his faith in her. It is an act of imagination, such as Williams acknowledged to lie also at the heart of "Deep Religious Faith" (1954; *CP2*: 262–63). In his poem of that title, Williams admonished his fellow poets not to allow their fascination with the results of "the 'laboratory' " to distract them from the underlying principle that also makes "the poet's line /come true" and creates the truth of the saints painted by El Greco, or, one might add, by Brueghel.

In *Paterson* 4, as Williams continues his presentation of the imaginative activity that unites the Curies, he arrives at the point of assigning it a name: love. Once again, however, he withholds his endorsement from that designation and instead offers his reader an alternative: "Love, the sledge that smashes the atom? No, No! antagonistic cooperation is the key, says Levy."[9] As in the case of Mariani's reading of what "the Italians say," Henry Sayre mistakes Williams's allusion to a "saying," in this case by Levy, as an appeal to authority and assumes that Williams is rejecting love in favor of "antagonistic cooperation" (*VT* 111–12). Each critic prefers what appears to be, quite literally, the "sexier" alternative: adultery rather than Virgin Birth, in Mariani's case; the perpetual tensions of the sexual relation rather than a love that resolves tension, in Sayre's case.[10] But construing Williams's questions in this way poses a new set of alternatives, neither of which preserves the kind of dualism that Williams regarded as truly sexual. On the one hand, sexuality is reduced to a mere theme in a structurally sexless text; the alternatives that Williams poses are understood to be false, permitting in fact only one predetermined choice. On the other hand, if Williams's alternatives are granted to be genuine, his text is accorded a kind of sexuality in which one of the terms must ultimately emerge as master.

In contrast to either of these alternatives, an "antagonistic cooperation" that does not privilege antagonism would allow for cooperation between the two terms that Williams offers. Neither term would be reduced to the other, but the stability of their separate identities would be shaken by an "interpenetration, both ways," such as Williams announces in the Preface to *Paterson* (*P* 3). As a result, it would appear that antagonistic cooperation *is* the key, but love is also capable of smashing the atom, as Williams suggests in a series of images of gentle force running throughout his work: "Saxifrage is my flower that splits / the rock."[11] As for the case of Joseph, the "Italians" are right to take the Baby born to his wife as proof that she has taken a lover. But Joseph is aware of that fact, just as Pierre Curie was aware of his wife's scientific experiments. Just as those experiments proved that "Dissonance / . . . leads to discovery" (*P* 176), Joseph has discovered, as Williams had, that "a marriage might be invigorated by deliberately breaking the vows" (*SE* 188). Thus invigorated, Joseph's continued attachment to his wife is not a sign that he has been duped by a myth of sexless procreation.

The extent to which that myth has duped Williams's critics will be evident if we turn now to the Epiphany scene in *Paterson* 5. This scene is frequently read as an allegory of artistic creation, much as I am proposing an allegory of artistic reception through the analogy between the relation of Joseph to Mary and the relation of reader to text. My objection to previous critics is that their model of artistic creation does not recognize a relation of partners but instead assumes works of art to spring "fresh and . . . virginal . . . from the head of their creator," in Paul Mariani's words.[12] In Mariani's reading of the Epiphany scene, the figure of the artist is, appropriately enough, the Virgin herself. On this aesthetic plane, her involvement with a lover is important only as an occasion for artistic invention. Because Mary has invented a story about her Baby's birth in order to fool her husband, she is an artist. But because she is herself the subject of her own fiction, she is also a work of art. In Mariani's summation, she is "the woman as artist, generator of myths who is herself generated by myth" (*NWN* 709). As in Church history, so in Mariani's poetics, the mother's Immaculate Conception becomes implicated in the Virgin Birth of her offspring.[13]

Jerome Mazzaro offers a variant of this immaculate aesthetic that is important because Williams's aesthetic theory concerns Mazzaro more centrally than it does Mariani, who is mainly concerned with Williams's life. Devoting an entire chapter to the topic of "Sex and the Williams Poem," Mazzaro attempts to give full recognition to the sexual component in Williams's aesthetic. In the course of that chapter, however, Mazzaro's emphasis on androgyny seems to define a position for which Williams criticized Pound, and which later critics of Pound have identified with the doctrine of Immaculate Conception.[14] Then, at the end of the chapter, Mazzaro posits a distinction between sex and intellect (*LP* 143), a distinction for which he finds little support in Williams, but which nevertheless provides the framework for the next chapter's examination of *Paterson* 5 and *Pictures from Brueghel*, where "the emphasis is to be put not on the poems or their sexuality but on the intelligence shaping the poems" (*LP* 150).

Thus, when Mazzaro arrives at the Epiphany scene in *Paterson* 5, he discovers that shaping intelligence in a male figure of the artist, represented by Joseph, through whose agency language, represented by the Baby, is rescued from the accretions of past usage, reborn into a new life (*LP* 161). This interpretation leads Mazzaro to conclude, against most critics, that Joseph is the father of the Baby, but Mazzaro does not postulate a sexual relation between Joseph and Mary. Mary "is completely ignored by Williams' stabilizing forces," Mazzaro claims, thus ignoring, in his turn, the fact that Williams refers to the mother as often as he does to the Baby, and plants the Baby stably "on his Mother's / knees." Although Williams mentions the Virgin prominently, Mazzaro's claim that he does not is modified by a suggestive observation to which I will want to return: "for Williams the Virgin is both the still center of the panel and the whole panel, and by speaking as he does of the entire panel, he is, though not mentioning her, in effect delineating her." In the immediate context of Mazzaro's argument, however, this observation is enlisted in the service of his immaculate aesthetic, in which Mary plays the role of the Holy Ghost. As "the artistic process," she produces a Baby by descending on Joseph, the virgin artist.

To his credit, Mazzaro indicates that he is not entirely happy with the view of the artistic process that emerges in his reading of the Epiphany scene. His dissatisfaction reflects his sense that the general direction of *Paterson* increasingly threatens to wander from the type of sexual relationship on which it was originally modeled. "The continuity was not conceived originally as male to male," or father to son, Mazzaro notes (*LP* 70). Rather, Williams had set out to establish the reciprocity of male and female, the "marriage" that is the solution to "The riddle of a man and a woman" (*P* 106). Mazzaro is right, I think, to emphasize the inconsistency in Williams's aesthetic (*LP* 146–47). However, he does not recognize the degree to which such inconsistency is an integral part of the aesthetic, rather than merely a flaw within it.[15] The degree of reciprocity that Williams permits in the relation of reader to text inevitably produces inconsistency, or "difference," as Williams calls it when, in "Pictures from Brueghel," he considers the London *Adoration* as a product of Brueghel's reading of "the Italian masters." But for Mazzaro, in contrast to Williams, readers should defer to the "masters," who are alone responsible for the texts they produce. Thus, when Mazzaro considers the Epiphany scene in *Paterson* 5 as a product of Williams's reading of Brueghel, he objects "that Williams' use of Brueghel as a master whom a writer might imitate without going astray involved on Williams' part a great deal of distortion and self-deception" (*LP* 161). I would admit the distortion, but the self-deception, I would suggest, is mostly on the part of Mazzaro, who will not admit the degree to which his own desire to find consistency in Williams's text makes the inconsistency he discovers appear as failure.

Nevertheless, Mazzaro's willingness to admit the appearance of inconsistency permits him to observe accurately the difference between Williams's poem and Brueghel's painting, based on the position assigned to Joseph in the composition of each work. Unlike Mariani, for whom the Virgin sits at the center of both painting and poem, and ultimately, "at the center of Williams' imagination" (*NWN* 709), Mazzaro recognizes Williams's poem to "center dually" on Joseph and the Baby.[16] The painting's focus on a single center, in which I would include both the Baby and his mother, is unusual for Brueghel, who more typically distracted attention from his compositional center or, as in *Landscape with the Fall of Icarus* (fig. 12), separated the compositional center from the narrative center proposed by the painting's "text."

The forceful centering of the London *Adoration* appears to be acknowledged by Williams. His description of the painting opens by centering the Baby "among the words," and then, after a fuller description of the Soldiers, returns at line 20, with the word "but," to a contrasting description of the Baby and his mother. Thus, Williams seems to evoke the periphery as a foil to the jewel in the center, much as Brueghel does. While thus respecting Brueghel's composition, however, Williams overlays it with a new composition of his own, producing the curious effect of a double exposure. In repeated statements, Williams insists that the center is occupied by Joseph, "the potbellied / greybeard (center)," "the old man in the / middle."

No single viewpoint within the poem can be held responsible for assigning this centrality to Joseph, because he is the focal point of a number of viewpoints, although for different reasons. To the Soldiers, he is "the butt of their comments" because they consider him a cuckold. To the Wise Men, on other hand, he is one member of the pair whom they seek to honor with their gifts, at least according to Williams. "How else to honor / an old man, or a woman?" Williams asks.

In contrast to the Soldiers' suspicions, Williams's question implies some sort of partnership between the Old Man and the woman. Paradoxically, the nature of that partnership depends on the very fact that provides grounds for the Soldiers' suspicion: the fact that the man is old. Williams insists on that fact as often as he insists on the Old Man's centrality.[17]

Just as Mazzaro's analysis is useful in pointing out that centrality, it is useful also for recognizing Joseph as one instance of "the 'old man' image of the artist." That figure appears in various guises throughout Williams's work, including, Mazzaro suggests, in the "Self-Portrait" that opens the "Pictures from Brueghel" sequence (*LM* 162; see fig. 7). Like other commentators, Mazzaro understands that poem, originally subtitled "The Old Shepherd," to be intended as Williams's "Self-Portrait" as much as Brueghel's, and it seems likely that a similar identification, also encouraged by the factor of age, operates in the case of Joseph.[18] Williams was seventy-two when he began *Paterson* 5, seventy-five when he wrote "Pictures from Brueghel." The infirmity of old age had fallen upon him suddenly, when he suffered the first of a series of strokes within the year after the completion of *Paterson* 4. His determination to write *Paterson* 5 must be understood at least in part as his defiance of the double threat of creative and sexual impotence.[19] Identification with Joseph, in particular, provided a means of exploring the possibility of

> a counter stress,
> > born of the sexual shock,
> > > which survives it, (*CP2*: 249)

as Williams expressed it in another poem of this period, "To Daphne and Virginia" (1953). Like the imagery of penetration in the passage from "Asphodel" quoted at the opening of this chapter, the imagery of "To Daphne and Virginia" suggests that sexual tension survives the loss of sexual contact, even as marriage survives, both for Williams, in "Asphodel," and for Joseph, in *Paterson* 5.

Such an analysis assigns a more central role to the mechanism of identification than it plays in Mazzaro's treatment of Williams's Old Man figure. For Mazzaro, the Old Man is important as a symbol of what the artist might be, ideally, rather than what a particular artist is in a specific set of biographical circumstances. To uncover the meaning of the ideal symbol, Mazzaro refers his readers to Jung's archetypes of the collective unconscious, specifically that of the "wise old man," who points to the unconscious as a source of knowledge and power when conscious resources threaten to prove inadequate.[20] An advantage of this approach is that it encourages recognition of the Old Man figure at earlier stages of Williams's career. The figure of Joseph, we will remember, appears in *Paterson* 4, before Williams had suffered his first stroke in 1951. However, the self-effacement that Joseph represents in *Paterson* 4, together with Williams's demotion of the three Wise Men in the Epiphany scene, discussed in chapter 3, makes it seem unlikely that Williams would want to promote Joseph for his wisdom. True, in his 1930 essay "Caviar and Bread Again," Williams praised Jung's notion of the artist's role as spiritual leader of the race, but such praise sounds hollow in the context of Williams's statements elsewhere about his own role, including his remark to John Thirlwall, "I never wanted to be separated from my fellow mortals by acting like an artist."[21]

In the immediate context of "Caviar and Bread Again," Jung seems to offer Williams the only available alternative to the view of art as a special form of repression, which is how Williams, along with Jung, interpreted the Freudian theory of sublimation. However, in contrast to Jung's view that the artist, as artist, is "neither auto, hetero, nor generally erotic"—a view that fully accords with Mazzaro's picture of Joseph as artist—Williams, as artist, experienced a very different alternative to Freudian sublimation.[22] Rather than repressing sexual energy, art served to release it. In Williams's treatment of the Epiphany scene, Joseph, who "gave up his work," and the Wise Men, who gave up their gold, become analogues not through the knowledge they contain but the energy they release.[23]

If, according to Williams, the Wise Men direct their gifts to both Joseph and Mary, Joseph's gift is directed more particularly to Mary. We can go much further in understanding their relationship by taking advantage of the convergence of recent Freudian theory with Williams's view of art as release. The possibility of such a convergence seems to have been recognized by Williams in a 1951 interview, when he acknowledged Freud's relevance to his own discovery that writing "relieves the feeling of distress." Williams continued: "I think quite literally, psychologically, speaking as Freud might think, that writing has meant that to me all the way through" (*Int* 8). Jacques Lacan supposed he had been the first to notice that "Freud might think" differently about the topic of sublimation than he had been understood to think, that in fact "sublimation is . . . satisfaction of the drive, without repression."[24] Following up on that suggestion, Julia Kristeva has elaborated a view of art as "a sublimated celebration of incest," in which the artist's desire finds satisfaction in an identification with the satisfaction, the jouissance, of an imagined mother (*TL* 253; cf. *DL* 242). This formulation takes one back to *In the American Grain* and "the dangerous ground of pleasure" (*IAG* 176), against which the various figures of the Epiphany scene arrange themselves in an intelligible pattern.

Joseph's place in that pattern emerges most clearly in a remarkable poem, predating *Paterson*, entitled "Thinking Back Toward Christmas: A Statement for the Virgin" (1944). It establishes the relation between Joseph and Mary on the basis of Williams's identification with the woman whom Paul Mariani calls "Williams' essential muse" (*NWN* 8), his paternal grandmother. Since it has only recently been included among Williams's *Collected Poems*, and since it bears on my concerns in nearly every detail, the poem is worth quoting in full:

> With sharp lights winking
> yellow, red
> in the early dawn
> in the darkness
> through the broom of branches—
> the world is gloomy and new
> and mostly silent
>
> Low to the left,
> beyond the hill, the sparkle
> of small lights
> upon a vague, milky ground—
> and higher, through a screen
> of dark catalpa husks,
> smooth, brokenly
> tilted to one sun-like star
> the moon
>
> The old man wakes early
> while married lovers
> lie abed
> and croaks his advice to
> all mothers: Be silent,

forbearing under the stars
but mostly silent,
silent as the dawn

And, adds the superannuated
carpenter—while
in the semi-dark a huge squirrel
runs leaping
through the snow: Dry leaves
at noon out of the wind
to lie in will
still stand a man in good stead.   (*CP2*: 49)

Once our eyes have adjusted to the dim light, we can recognize in these lines the principal characters of a Nativity scene. Joseph is the easiest to recognize, as "the superannuated / carpenter," "the old man," who is identified by the same phrase in *Paterson* 5. The Virgin is named explicitly in the title. In the poem, however, because Joseph seems to have withdrawn an even greater distance from her than he does in *Paterson* 5, her outline has been generalized to that of "all mothers," to whom Joseph addresses his words of advice. In contrast to Jerome Mazzaro's analysis of the Epiphany scene in *Paterson* 5, the Virgin, rather than the Baby, remains Joseph's object, yet the manner in which her presence suffuses the landscape supports Mazzaro's sense of such a suffusion in *Paterson* 5. In the earlier poem, one can still specifically identify the female imagery that pervades the scene, from the "vague, milky ground" to the moon in the sky, and perhaps even to the "one sun-like star," which may be the "morning star," Venus, though it doubtless also recalls the biblical star that guided the Wise Men to the Epiphany scene.[25] They have not yet arrived in "Thinking Back Toward Christmas," however, where the birth itself appears to be still in progress. As identified in chapter 2, the Baby is "the world . . . gloomy and new," whose outline is just beginning to emerge from the "milky ground" of the mother.

The "fluid identity" provided by such a ground, in the deliberately punning terms of Julia Kristeva (*TL* 256), makes the child difficult to distinguish from the mother but at the same time permits identification across the division of sexual difference. Suspecting that "It is the woman in us / That makes us write," in his early poem "Transitional" (1914; *CP1*: 40), Williams attributed to the artist especially a bisexual (not androgynous) consciousness "of the two sides," like that which he claimed in *Paterson* 5 for Brueghel, who "saw it / from the two sides." On the same principle, "those saints that were womanly, or, like St. Francis, full of compassion" provide a model for marriage in *The Build-Up*. In "Thinking Back Toward Christmas," identification across sexual difference sustains the marriage between the Virgin and Joseph, though he no longer keeps either the hours or the bed of "married lovers."

Some sort of relationship between Joseph and the Virgin is maintained through his speech, which is addressed to her. The substance of the speech moves the relationship in the direction of identification. Why would Joseph conclude his "advice to / all mothers" by observing what will "stand a man in good stead," unless the point of his advice is to "be like me"—be "forbearing"? The complementary instruction, to be silent, initially appears contradictory; it would seem to recommend that the Virgin be *un*like Joseph, who breaks silence as he speaks. In fact, however, this point reveals the most profound level of identification operating in the poem. The words "Be mostly silent" are spoken by the "Marvellous old queen" who initiates the novice poet in Williams's early poem of vocation, "The Wanderer."[26] Identifying the old woman as an "idealization" of his grandmother, Williams explained further that "I identified my grandmother with my poetic unconscious" (*Int* 76). That Williams chooses his grandmother for this role rather than his mother is not a problem that need concern us, as it has other readers.[27] Williams also incorporates one of his mother's favorite words, "rococo" (*IWWP* 25), in the subtitle of "The Wanderer," "A Rococo Study." Like Joseph in "Thinking Back Toward Christmas," Williams identifies with "all mothers" through the act of speech, particularly poetic speech, whose peculiarly fluid treatment of the identities normally fixed by grammar seems to derive from the poet's ideal mother as much as the infant's milk derives from the real mother.[28]

At this point, acknowledging an objection on feminist grounds to Williams's use of women's words will help us in drawing conclusions about the special kind of relationship that Williams posits between man and woman, poem and painting, and reader and text. Sandra Gilbert has charged that Williams, as a reader of women's texts, reveals an anxiety that she holds to be typical of male modernist writers, who, "trapped in a unique sexual dialectic, . . . may well have worried that even the most extravagant techniques of ventriloquism, usurpation, and symbolization could not save them from the authentic anger or the potenial power of vengeful women."[29] I examined the charge of symbolization in the previous chapter, in the case of the Beautiful

Thing. Now, however, we are confronted with a case of possible ventriloquism that would also be usurpation. Certainly, by pretending to offer advice to "all mothers" through their own words, Joseph, in "Thinking Back Toward Christmas," would seem to have usurped the position of authority to which their words might entitle them if they were allowed to speak for themselves. Does the process of identification that is at work here involve more than a desire to join the Mother in the place that she occupies? Is it also a desire to displace her?

The answer is yes, if identification has the meaning that it has for Sandra Gilbert, who derives it from the theory of poetic influence elaborated by Harold Bloom. He, in turn, derives it from Freud's view of the role played by identification in Oedipal rivalry, where the son's identification with the father becomes a symbolic substitute for parricide.[30] The particular mode of this aggression is determined by an earlier stage of psychic development, however. Freud postulated that identification originates in the oral stage, specifically in the infant's desire to devour its object, which at first is the mother's breast. Hence, Gilbert refers to Williams's "voracious consumption" of women's words.[31]

As with the case of sublimation, that of identification has been undergoing reexamination in post-Lacanian psychoanalysis, as part of a broader effort to pursue lines of inquiry only begun in some of Freud's more speculative moments. Freud attempted to distinguish identification from libidinal attachment to an object by calling the former a mode of "being," while the latter was a mode of "having," or what I have been calling possession.[32] What Gilbert calls Williams's "usurpation" of women's words would be an attempt to possess those words and would acquire its violent tenor from that fact as much as from its role in the Oedipal rivalry of father and son, after the mother has emerged for the son as an object of libidinal attachment. The difficulty of conceiving a relationship that is not a form of possession is the difficulty that Freud's followers have found in trying to conceive an identification with something that is not an object, as psychoanalysis usually understands that term. Compounding the difficulty of bringing this "nonobject" into focus is the psychic stage at which it comes into play.[33] It would be a stage prior to the recognition of any sexual difference, as Freud had been led to conclude in other contexts. Hence, the "primary identification" that Freud postulates at this stage engages with both parents before they are clearly differentiated. A "father of individual prehistory," as Freud mysteriously calls him, serves as the point of orientation, but that point is simultaneously the place that the mother occupies for the infant.

From Freud's hints, and from her own experience as a psychoanalyst, Julia Kristeva has conceived of a type of identification that bears to Freud's Oedipal type the kind of paradoxical relation of interpenetrating difference that Williams's "love" bears to Levy's "antagonistic cooperation." "Love" is in fact the name Kristeva gives to the type of identification she postulates. Because the infant is at first unaware of sexual difference, the "father of individual prehistory" with whom the infant identifies is "the same as 'both parents' " (*TL* 26), and the violence of Oedipal rivalry with one parent for possession of the other remains in the future. Already, however, this archaic stage of the psyche has a past, for it has put behind it the violence with which primary narcissism maintained self-possession and imagines instead a "harmonious identification with the Loved One, accessible beyond violence" (*TL* 166). "For me to have been capable of such a process," Kristeva explains, "my libido had to be restrained; my thirst to devour had to be deferred and displaced [that is, sublimated] to a level one may well call 'psychic,' provided one adds that if there is repression it is quite primal, and that it lets one hold on to the joys of chewing, swallowing, nourishing oneself" (*TL* 26).

But why is such chewing and swallowing not just another form of taking possession of an object through violence? Kristeva's answer is to take Freud at his word, and to consider the possibility of a form of relationship that does not relate to an object by "having it" but that relates instead to a "nonobject" by "being like" it. I enter such a relation, according to Kristeva, if what I chew and swallow are words. "On what ground," Kristeva asks, "within what material does *having* switch over to *being*? While seeking an answer to that question it appeared to me that incorporating and introjecting orality's function is the essential substratum of what constitutes man's being, namely, *language*. When the object that I incorporate is the speech of the other—precisely a nonobject, a pattern, a model—I bind myself to him [who is simultaneously her] in a primary fusion, communion, unification. An identification" (*TL* 26).

As long as language, then, remains the medium of exchange, Williams's relation to women need not be the antagonistic one assumed by Sandra Gilbert. But the centrality that Kristeva assigns to language lends urgency to another of Gilbert's charges against Williams, this time conceived not on the model of reader to text but of poem to painting. Rather than facing the challenge of appropriating women's texts, according to Gilbert, Williams would prefer to exclude women from the realm of language altogether by conferring upon them the silence of visual art: "Caught motionless in a photograph," for instance, "the chief's wives [in *Paterson* 1 (*P* 13)] become hieroglyphs of a meaning that they cannot themselves articulate; rather, the poet will go on, as he later does, to articulate it *for* them, or perhaps more accurately, to attribute it *to* them."[34] Although Joseph's paradoxical use of speech to advise "all mothers" to be silent might be understood in this light, such an understanding depends on the assumption that speech, articulation, is the only outlet for meaning, an assumption that Williams does not share with Gilbert.

Gilbert's equation of meaning and speech is a tendency that Williams recognized to be typical of the literary person, whose view of visual art is accordingly distorted, even when the viewer also practices the art. In paintings by the poet E. E. Cummings, Williams suspected, "it is what the paintings literally *say* that is important to Mr. Cummings. That can be of no importance to a painter, only the design—and the color, the same thing, the inarticulate design" (*RI* 233). According to the principle of "design," an artist like Cézanne could "put it down on the canvas so that there would be a meaning without saying anything at all" (*Int* 53). By application of that principle to poetry, "it is not by what the poem says that we have the greatness of art," Williams claimed. "It is by what the poem has been made to *be* that we recognize it."[35] But that being was still a form of meaning. Archibald MacLeish's famous disjunction of being and meaning would be no more acceptable to Williams than Sandra Gilbert's conjunction of meaning and saying.

Thus, the rule of silence in which Joseph instructs women, and that Williams derived from a woman, remains compatible with the role of language in the process of identification described by Julia Kristeva. In that process, language operates at a level that is not symbolic but rather psychosomatic, or "semiotic," as Kristeva calls it (*RPL* 28). It embodies "a significance . . . that is prior to the sign" (*TL* 84), and is thus "inarticulate" in the very precise sense that "the linguistic sign is not yet articulated as the absence of an object" (*RPL* 26). Prelinguistic in origin, the semiotic dimension is especially noticeable in areas situated either outside or at the margins of traditional linguistic analysis: in visual art, particularly in color; in poetic language, particularly in rhythm; and in "women's discourse," particularly in intonation.[36]

However, in Kristeva's semiotic analysis, these activities are understood to function not apart from or simply prior to language, but in a special relation to language that is literally "para-doxical," that is, placed against those functions of language that express *doxa* or social norms (*RPL* 27, 82). In Kristeva's sense, as an ordering but not a normative principle, paradox pervades Williams's aesthetic: from the notion of design that means without saying, to Joseph's use of speech to recommend silence; from the notion of love that can split the atom, to Joseph's separation from Mary as a form of love.

If love is a mode of identification, however, how does it include separation? This final challenge to Williams's, and Kristeva's, position comes from the theoretical perspective of Jacques Lacan, who also characterizes visual art as a trap, located outside language, but for a reason different from Sandra Gilbert's. Visual experience in general comes under suspicion in Lacanian analysis because it is the vehicle for a profound confusion that Lacan associates with primary narcissism, the stage at which Lacan also locates primary identification. Because the infant at this stage is thought to be unable to sense its separation from what it sees, principally the mother, Lacan symbolizes this condition by the mirror, and calls the condition itself "specular," after the Latin word for mirror, *speculum*.[37]

The role played in Williams's writing by the figure of the mother, as noted here and in the preceding chapter, would furnish abundant evidence for a narcissistic orientation in this psychoanalytic sense, and additional evidence could easily be furnished. The well-known poem "Danse Russe" (1916; *CP1*: 86–87), in which the poet dances naked before his mirror, exults in his loneliness, and declares himself "the happy genius of my household," reads like a reenactment of Lacan's "mirror stage." In contrast, the "search for the redeeming language" that motivates *Paterson* could be read as a search for separation from the mother, in view of the role that Lacan assigns to language, whose symbolic function enters with the "name of the father" to break up the mother-child dyad during the Oedipal stage.[38] However, in *Paterson* 5, a book conceived as a celebration of women, the father that Williams presents is Joseph, who hardly produces an impression of phallic authority.[39] Rather, he functions in the manner that Julia Kristeva describes for the pre-Oedipal "father of individual prehistory," who moderates the fusional tendencies of the mother-child dyad not through absolute separation, maintained through the threat of castration posed by the Oedipal father, but rather through the promise of love.

The possibility of loving one other than oneself appears as a novel prospect on the horizon of the realm of Narcissus. Kristeva reasons that the possibility must present itself first not within the infant subject but within those shadowy figures that have not yet taken on definition as objects. Thus, the subject first discovers not his own love for another but the other's love for a Third Party, or the mother's love for the father. Embracing both of these figures, primary identification is oriented not so much toward a loved object as toward the act of love, as a form of relationship.[40] Rather than posing as a rival for a love that the subject wants to keep focused on himself, the Third Party opens up the very possibility of being loved: because she could love him, she could also love me (*TL* 34).

Within the story that Williams tells about Joseph, he occupies the place that Kristeva would assign to the infant in the structure of primary identification. His love for Mary is based on an identification with her love for another, whether that be the Baby or the absent lover (cf. *TL* 261). Joseph functions as the father in Kristeva's scenario only within the story that Williams tells about Brueghel's painting. By using Joseph to add a second center to the composition, Williams prevents the painting from exercising the specular fascination that Lacan attributes to visual art. According to Lacan, such fascination occurs if the point from which the viewer perceives the painting is experienced, narcissistically, as the only possible viewpoint, an experience encouraged by the construction of geometric perspective. In a discussion of Holbein's *Ambassadors* (1533; fig. 13), Lacan demonstrates the disruption of such perspective by the introduction of an anamorphic object, in this case a skull, which can be perceived intelligibly only from a viewpoint different from that required to perceive the rest of the painting.[41] Williams assigns to Joseph the function that Lacan assigns to the skull. Though he claims that "Peter Brueghel the artist saw it / from the two sides," Williams himself is responsible for locating Joseph in a second center within the painting, perceivable as such only from a viewpoint other than that which assigns centrality to the mother and Baby.

Of course, in symbolic value, Joseph is very different from a skull, however similar they may be in their structural function. The skull was obviously a symbol of death for Holbein. For Lacan, it threatens death to the narcissistic viewer because it represents that which he is not, or that where he is not, to speak in spatial terms more suited to the picture. Joseph, on the other hand, represents the possibility of being in that other place through an act of identification, and hence of coming into being as a subject for that other: "you love me therefore I am" (*TL* 227). In contrast to Holbein's skull, such a love poses a "magical challenge to death," according to Kristeva (*TL* 233), who thus designates precisely the challenge that Williams declares in "Asphodel":

> love and the imagination
> > are of a piece,
> > > swift as the light
> to avoid destruction.   (*CP2*: 334)

Neither Williams nor Kristeva would deny the imaginary nature of that challenge, but both would insist on the need for creating a space for the imagination, to which one might withdraw to gather energy for a renewed encounter with reality.

Both Kristeva and Williams depict that special therapeutic space as the space of marriage. For Williams, it is the marriage of Mary and Joseph in the Epiphany scene, or his own marriage, as he imagines it in "Asphodel." For Kristeva, it is the meeting of analyst and analysand in the psychoanalytic transference, or the union of Romeo and Juliet, after their death, as Kristeva imagines it in *Tales of Love*. In her analysis of Shakespeare's play, Kristeva makes it clear that the lovers' tragedy is caused not only by social restrictions but also by their own passion, founded, in Kristeva's psychoanalytic perspective, on the death drive. But the imaginary refiguring of death as the sleep of lovers holds that drive in abeyance. "Without the representation of the lovers' union, sleeping in each other's arms, erotic expenditure is a race toward death," Kristeva comments. "The sleep of lovers, moreover, merely refills a stock of imaginative energy that is ready, at the wakening, for new expenditures, new caresses, under the sway of the senses. . . Romeo and Juliet, in their sleeping death, are, like our sleep together when we are in love, a stock of fusional images that assuage erotic frenzy for a while before stimulating it again. . . " (*TL* 233). In *A Novelette* (1932), when Williams's wife asks him, "Why do you write?" he replies, "For relaxation, relief. To have nothing in my head,—to freshen my eye by that till I see, smell, know and can reason and be" (*I* 289). Later, he tells her, "You, I, we, cannot you see how in the singleness of these few days marriage and writing have been fused . . . ?" (*I* 294).

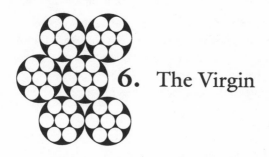

6. The Virgin

THE FUSION of marriage and writing that Williams proclaims in *A Novelette* is not merely an equation of the two institutions. The writing simultaneously sustains and undoes the marriage. It is the "hard work" of the imagination by which the writer "unmarries" husband and wife, in the terms employed by Doc Thurber, Williams's persona in the play *A Dream of Love* (1948; *ML* 200). This work produces an image such as Williams celebrates in *Paterson* 5:

> —every married man carries in his head
> > the beloved and sacred image
> > > of a virgin
> whom he has whored   (*P* 234)

He has whored her because he has married her, but the image he carries in his head preserves her as a virgin, "made of pure consents," to use again the language of *A Dream of Love*. Her virginity, in other words, consists in her consenting without the constraints of marriage vows. "But surely," one is tempted to object, "she suffers enough constraint in having to exist 'in his head.'" In a process that Doc Thurber's wife, Myra, bluntly describes as "rape," the woman appears to be completely subordinated to the meaning the man assigns to her, as the object of his interpretation. *Paterson* 5 supplies an answer to these objections. The "pure consent" in which virginity consists depends on the object's ability to exceed interpretation.

Even more so than in previous chapters, the problem of interpretation will seem to eclipse the object proposed as the focus of this chapter, the Virgin Mary as she appears in Williams's poems. As Julia Kristeva has argued in the case of the many Madonnas painted by Giovanni Bellini, I will argue that the Virgin, for Williams, stands at "the limits of representability" (*DL* 269). In *Paterson* 5, she is one of a series of female figures who provocatively elude the gaze of the male observer identified as Paterson. The series includes the "woman in our town," who stops Paterson in his tracks, only to "disappear in the crowd" (P 219); Leonardo's *Mona Lisa* (ca. 1503–5), with her famous enigmatic smile (P 222); and the woman in the Unicorn tapestries, "lost in the woods (or hiding)," who interests Paterson "by her singularity" (P 237; fig. 14). In the Epiphany scene that Williams bases on Brueghel's painting, the Virgin's place is more central than that of any figure other than Joseph, yet it seems impossible to focus on her. The gifts of the Wise Men are intended "to honor / an old man, or a woman," yet even as she is being honored, the Virgin appears to hover just at the border of the statement, almost as if her inclusion were an afterthought. A similar impression is produced by the statement that the Baby has been,

> born to an old man
> out of a girl and a pretty girl
> at that,

where the girl only gradually commands our attention, and then disappears from our sight as soon as she has done so.

This pattern is confirmed if the scope of attention is enlarged to include Williams's other poems dealing with the Virgin. As suggested in the preceding chapter, "Thinking Back Toward Christmas" is conceived in its entirety as a "Statement for the Virgin," yet her image is diffused into "a vague, milky ground" (*CP2*: 49). Grammatically, throughout this series of poems, the Virgin tends to occupy the attributive rather than the substantive position, and even the rare substantive form serves as nominalized attribution, as in the vague gesture toward "this perfection" at the close of "The Gift." We catch a glimpse of a more particularized figure only through references to "a mother's needs" or "a mother's milk," in "The Gift"; "his Mother's knees," in *Paterson* 5; or "its Mother's arms," in "Pictures from Brueghel." The only other reference to the Virgin in this last poem floats in grammatical suspension in the final stanza, and the image it describes, "the downcast eyes of the Virgin," is itself one of evasion. The cumulative effect of these various evasive strategies is perhaps best summed up in "For Eleanor and Bill Monahan" (*CP2*: 252–55), the poem in which Williams addresses the Virgin in his own voice, but confesses,

> As far as spring is
>> from winter
>>> so are we
> from you now.

Williams's adaptation of the Virgin's traditional function as intercessor complicates the difficulty of looking at her, since we are constantly invited to look *through* her to some other object, from whom Williams seeks forgiveness. In "For Eleanor and Bill Monahan," God the Father is present in a reference to "His rule," but Williams's appeal is to "The female principle of the world," because his immediate need is to be forgiven by his wife, "she to whom I cling." Dedicated to friends whose Catholic faith inspired Williams's appeal to the Virgin, the poem was written in December 1952, as Williams was slipping into a deep depression following his stroke in August of that year.[1] With the end of his life thus brought sharply into focus, Williams felt the need to confess to his wife his history of infidelity. She was evidently shaken by his disclosures, and Williams feared to see "both / of us go down" unless she could forgive him.

The ground of his hope is evident in an image that Williams employed both in the Monahan poem and in "Asphodel, That Greeny Flower"; it is difficult to say where the image appeared first, since at the time of the shorter poem's composition Williams had begun but not yet completed "Asphodel." Addressing the Virgin of the Monahans, Williams tells how,

> I have seen you stoop
>> to a merest flower
> and raise it
>> and press it to your cheek.

Addressing his wife in "Asphodel," Williams describes her tending her plants,

>> as you compassionately
> pour at their roots
>> the reviving water.
>>> Lean-cheeked
> I say to myself
>> kindness moves her
>>> shall she not be kind
> also to me?

(*CP2*: 330)

The psychic mechanism operating here is precisely that form of identification to which Kristeva credits the first awakening to the possibility of love. The relation is triangular from the start: I identify with her through her love for him. If she could love him—or it (the flower)—she can also love me (*TL* 34).

The fluidity of sexual identities that accompanies this mechanism, discussed in the preceding chapter, suggests that the translation between biographical model and poetic image will not always be so straightforward. Indeed, if a man carries his image of his wife "in his head," its priority as model over other images contained there is open to question. In "The Mental Hospital Garden" (*CP2*: 264–67), apparently written while Williams was receiving institutional treatment for the same depression that gave birth to the Monahan poem, the figure from whom the poet seeks forgiveness for "all lovers" is St. Francis, whom Williams's persona in *The Build-Up* proposes as the model for his marriage. Like Floss as she tends her plants in "Asphodel," St. Francis is "womanly, or . . . full of compassion" (*BU* 263). In *Paterson* 5, the compassionate figure is Joseph, whose task is to forgive the passion of his spouse. On the biographical plane, then, Williams could identify Floss with Joseph at the same time that he identified with him himself, as the Old Man. But he could also identify himself with Joseph's wife, that "whore" whose infidelity Williams admits even as he maintains her virginity, just as he maintained, "in spite of the 'wrong note' / . . . My heart is / innocent," in another late poem addressed to his wife, "The Orchestra" (1952; *CP2*: 252).

Again as in the case of the Old Man, this whirlpool of identifications centered on the Virgin extends to depths that defy biographical measurement. It is more than a question of the poet's remorse in old age. While still in middle age, Williams was asking forgiveness of his mother in the poem "Eve" (1936), and her determination "to live always—unforgiving" (*CP1*: 413) carries us back even further to the Muse figure of "The Wanderer," whom Williams identified with his grandmother: "She of whom I told you, that old queen, / Forgiveless, unreconcilable!" (*CP1*: 28). Leading "all the persons of godhead" in her train (*CP1*: 28), that "old harlot" (*CP1*: 30) is the original virgin-whore in Williams's poetry, but it does not necessarily follow that Williams's grandmother is the original model for that image.[2] It would be more correct to say that grandmother, mother and wife, Flemish Virgin, Italian Mona Lisa and "singular" woman of the Cloisters tapestry, are all equally foreign to Williams's experience, all equally images of "another world," from which, like "A Negro Woman" (1955), each serves, in her own way, as "ambassador" (*CP2*: 287).

"Women remained an enigma," Williams explained toward the end of his life; "no two had the same interest for me; they were all different" (*IWWP* 64). What they shared was a gaze turned elsewhere, from the "averted" eyes of the Muse in "The Wanderer" (*CP1*: 35) to "the downcast eyes of the Virgin" in "Pictures from Brueghel." So, too, in the case of Bellini, Kristeva finds, "the faces of his Madonnas are turned away, intent on something else that draws their gaze to the side, up above, or nowhere in particular, but never centers it in the baby" (*DL* 247; fig. 15). They evoke "a space of fundamental unrepresentability toward which all glances nonetheless converge" (*DL* 249). Because he is bound to representation, Kristeva insists, the painter, for whom I would substitute the poet, "can never reach this elsewhere."[3]

This is why we will never reach the Virgin in this chapter, and why we will continue to pursue her through the problem of interpretation, that is, the problem of her unreachability. First, however, it is necessary to attend to the counterclaim that the only problem Williams presents to interpretation is his transparency; he seems to leave the interpreter nothing to do.[4] This position is grounded in the epistemological claim that there is no "elsewhere" for Williams, a claim that, in its most extreme form, is represented by Hillis Miller in his phenomenological phase, though it receives surprisingly little modification as Miller moves toward deconstruction. Miller argues that Williams managed to overcome subject-object dualism by abandoning his ego at the outset of his career, in a move symbolized by his leap into the Passaic River in "The Wanderer" (*PR* 11, 292; cf. *LM* 361). Thereafter, Williams enters the object that formerly he would have regarded from a distance. When people are the object in question, as is generally the case, for instance, in Williams's fiction, "he enters into people rather than into flowers or the river" (*PR* 323).

This model persists in a wide variety of critical perspectives on Williams's images of women. Women's "otherness," to which feminism has encouraged greater attention, is found to be reduced by Williams to "an 'otherness' available to *any* heroic man," in Sandra Gilbert's ironic formulation, or reduced from "the displaced alienated Other of Simone de Beauvoir and Julia Kristeva," in the more admiring judgment of Stephen Tapscott.[5] The difference between Gilbert's irony and Tapscott's admiration is a function of their different reading of

Williams's tone: aggressive, in Gilbert's reading; sympathetic, in Tapscott's. Both critics agree that the tone results from what Tapscott calls Williams's "experiments in writing about female sexuality from within a female character" (38), which presupposes an ability, such as Miller posits, to enter into the object. Even when a critic judges that Williams usually fails to "penetrate to the hidden, inner core" of a woman's being, such penetration is still assumed to be the goal. According to Kerry Driscoll, who states the goal in the words I have just quoted, Williams "*successfully* overcame his perception of female 'otherness' " only in his relation with his mother.[6] When she treats Williams's discussion of his mother's "detachment from the world of Rutherford" (9), Driscoll ignores Williams's more specific claim, that his mother was "remote" from him (*IWWP* 16).

To conceive even the possibility of the fusion with the object that Williams's critics assume for him, they must conceive an exchange with the object that is either immediate or conducted through a medium that is totally transparent. Hillis Miller stays close to the former position even in *The Linguistic Moment*, where the medium so boldly proclaimed in the title is permitted just "ever so slightly" to delay Williams's "return to the facts of immediate experience."[7] Stephen Tapscott more readily concedes Williams's dependence on mediation, as we might expect in the critic who has done more than any other to acknowledge inaccessibility as a factor in Williams's relation to women. "Their sexual inaccessibility to him," Tapscott argues, "requires Williams to find some other concept of conjunction, some erotic-but-not-sexual mediation of subject and object, some poetry of natural speech, that allows them a reciprocal voice" (40). In "natural speech," however, Tapscott thinks Williams found a transparent medium, one that allowed him verbally to penetrate the feminine mystery that remained sexually inaccessible to him.

In the process of valorizing "natural speech," or "voice," as a transparent medium, the concrete, hence potentially more opaque medium of visual art is either denied the difference of its concreteness or explicitly denigrated. Miller predictably aligns Williams with those developments in modern visual art that Miller interprets as developments toward immediacy (PR 9; LM 360). In the same statement on his mother in which Williams describes her remoteness from him, Kerry Driscoll notes the remark, "Her interest in art became my interest in art," but she gives no thought to the displacement between the mother's art, painting, and the son's, poetry. "In terms of her son's poetry," Driscoll argues, "Elena was most compellingly a voice" (9). I have already noted, in the preceding chapter, Sandra Gilbert's distrust of visual art as a suppression of voice. For Stephen Tapscott, the voice that Williams discovered in his late work marks an advance over "the visual, Cubist form" in which Williams composed the earlier books of *Paterson* (30).

In his attempt to arrange Williams's career as a progression from vision, or "writing," toward speech, Tapscott encounters a serious obstacle in *Paterson* 5, which other critics have read as Williams's culminating affirmation both of "writing" and visual art.[8] Indeed, many of the images of women in *Paterson* 5—Brueghel's Virgin, Leonardo's Mona Lisa, the "singular" woman in the tapestry—are presented through the medium of visual art. The moves by which Tapscott attempts to get around this obstacle seem contorted, as when he places "Asphodel," which he prefers, both at the origin of *Paterson* 5 and "later," when the dominance of speech is "finally" secured (39). In his most ingenious argument, however, Tapscott clearly exposes, if such a thing can ever be exposed, the transparency that he attributes to speech. Even when we are given no image of a woman in Williams's late work, she is still present for Tapscott, because Williams has "internalized that 'clear gentle voice' " he had heard in Sappho. Now the medium cannot obstruct Williams's access to the woman, because she *is* the medium.[9]

Williams said something like that, but in his case the medium was painting, and the point of identifying the medium with woman was to emphasize the impossibility of a man's fully "internalizing" either one. The text in question is "Woman as Operator," written in 1948 for an exhibition of paintings on the theme of woman. Williams takes Romare Bearden's *Women with an Oracle* (1947; fig. 16) as his point of departure, though not as an object for detailed analysis. Since its reprinting in 1978, Williams's essay has been criticized as "sexist" because it argues that woman is an appropriate subject for abstract art. Hence, it is held to deny women's capacity for individuation, or at least to encourage neglect of particularity in the portrayal of women, whether in visual art or poetry.[10] "Woman doesn't have to be so particularized" as man does, writes Williams. "With her, somehow, an intimate relationship blends itself into the material (paint)" (*RI* 180). Interpretation of this statement hinges on the verb "to be." If Williams is talking about the being of woman, then his critics' objections are justified. The context of the essay makes clear, however, that the critics have once again overlooked the process of representation as the subject to which Williams's remarks are directly addressed. He is not denying particularity to women. He is discussing alternative modes of representing that particularity in painting.

The question Williams confronts, then, is not, "What is the truth about woman?" but rather, "What is the truth about the way the artist sees her?" If the artist is a man, as were all the contributors to the exhibition on which Williams had been invited to comment, and as, of course, Williams himself was, a woman will present a very different object from another man. The man's experience will necessarily be conceived in terms of the world the artist shares with him, "what he does, what he knows, what he desires or makes" (RI 180), but the woman's experience will be simply unimaginable, Williams believes. She will remain Other despite the artist's desire to possess her, and even, more mysteriously, despite her own apparent willingness to be possessed. "To a man," Williams confesses, "the more loving and willing she is and the more she gives herself, the more remote she becomes to him."[11] By being a whore, she becomes all the more virgin, a condition Williams here characterizes as the "impossibility of a meeting between the sexes."[12]

The particularity of woman, then, does not reside in representational detail but rather in her peculiar relationship to the project of representation. As in the case of the woman in the Cloisters tapestry, whose "singularity" is enhanced by her "hiding" (P 237), "Woman as Operator" can "be particularized" by remaining virginal, "beyond his [the artist's] power" (RI 180–81)—the power, that is, of representation—at the same time that she offers herself to that power, like a whore. This is the "intimate relationship [that] blends itself into the material (paint)," partly, to be sure, because Williams was seduced by the sensual qualities of paint as he was by women, but also because the *relationship* between the artist and either paint or woman prevented seduction from closing in possession.

"That is what it is to be an artist with his material before him," Williams had declared in his essay on "French Painting" (RI 70). The material remains "before him," resisting the "internalization" to which Stephen Tapscott would submit "natural speech," but permitting identification with "the speech of the other," in Kristeva's terms (TL 26), precisely because the otherness remains. French painting had helped Williams to discover a quality of resistance in words analogous to that of paint: "Stein has stressed, as Braque did paint, words" (RI

70). On the other hand, Williams's experience of writing, whether Gertrude Stein's or his own, had taught him that emphasis on the medium marked the boundary of representation, the region where he found the image of woman. Paint placed on the canvas for its own sake could not escape representation entirely, any more than could the painted figure of a woman: "all painting is representational, even the most abstract."[13] Like woman, what abstraction represents is, paradoxically, the defiance of representation.

Abstraction had become the rallying cry of modern art, as Williams was well aware, but his understanding of abstraction as a particular relationship between the painter and his object, rather than as a particular "look" to a painting, meant that modern artists in pursuit of abstraction might find valuable lessons in the representational art of the past. "The *Melancholy* of Brueghel [*sic*], the use of gold by Fra Angelico or the works of Hieronymous Bosch are not to be ignored," Williams advised in a 1956 review.[14] In the section of *Paterson* 5 that Williams published separately as "Tribute to the Painters" (1955; *CP2*: 296–98), he correctly attributed the famous allegory of *Melancholy* (1514; fig. 17) to Dürer rather than Brueghel, but the point of the passage remains the continuity between modernism—Klee, Picasso, Gris—and the art of the past, as far back as "the abstraction / of Arabic art."[15]

That Brueghel, in Williams's view, has a rightful part in that continuity is confirmed in *Paterson* 5 by the proximity—a matter of two pages—between the lines of "Tribute to the Painters" and the section treating Brueghel's Epiphany scene. Williams's earlier confusion of Brueghel and Dürer illuminates the basis for that proximity. In Dürer's *Melancholy*, Williams thought he saw "shattered masonry" and "gears / lying disrelated to the mathematics of the / machine."[16] In Brueghel's Epiphany, Williams found a variety of "disrelations": between the central actors and the bystanders; between Mary and Joseph; and finally, between the painting and the artist, who portrayed the entire scene "dispassionately," according to Williams. In that disrelation, the artist is "passionate as one says of a saint" (*BU* 263). What distinguishes the modern artist from his predecessors, including the saint (*CP1*: 199), is not the condition of disrelation, which was always present, but rather the modern insistence on acknowledging that condition as one's own. It is, after all, the modern artist Williams who highlights Brueghel's relation to his painting so that Williams might focus on the problem of representation.

To maintain that focus, I want to turn now to a consideration of Williams's treatment of two modern paintings, one by Gauguin, the other by Matisse. This procedure will, I hope, eventually prove to involve less of a departure from the case of Brueghel than may at first appear. Both Gauguin's and Matisse's paintings depict female nudes whose virginity is as problematic for Williams as that of Mary in Brueghel's Epiphany scene. Having examined the difficulties of a direct approach to that figure, let us attempt, by studying her modern analogues, to approach her by indirection, or by that structure of "disrelation" that Brueghel's art, according to Williams, shares with modern painting.

The "unrelatedness" of the title of Gauguin's painting *The Loss of Virginity* (1890; fig. 19) is the subject of Williams's poem "The Title" (1956; *CP2*: 425), which reads in its entirety as follows:

> The Title
>
> —as in Gauguin's *The Loss of Virginity*—
> how inessential it is to the composition:
>
> the nude body, unattended save by a watchful
> hound, forepaw against the naked breast,
>
> there she lies on her back in an open field,
> limbs quietly assembled—yet how by its
>
> very unrelatedness it enhances the impact
> and emotional dignity of the whole . . .

Conventionally, the title identifies the object the painting seeks to represent. In Gauguin's painting, whose images do not literally depict a loss of virginity, the "unrelatedness" of title and image seems to mark a limit to representation, the limit that Williams called abstraction.[17]

Although Gauguin spoke of his work in terms of abstraction, interpreters have usually dealt with it in terms of symbolism, another term authorized by Gauguin, but not, as most interpreters employ it, for the purpose of pushing his work back from the border of representation into a realm of more secure meaning.[18] We do not have Gauguin's own interpretation of *The Loss of Virginity*, and in fact even the title only carries his "provisional" authorization. But we do have his explanation of a closely related painting, *The Spirit of the Dead Watching* (*Manao tupapau*) (1892; fig. 18), in which another female nude is watched over by an ominous figure, whose spiritual significance is made more explicit, both in the title and in the painting, than is that of the animal in *The Loss of Virginity*.[19] Such explicitness helps to sharpen but not to remove ambiguity. Gauguin explains, "The title *Manao tupapau* has two meanings, either the girl thinks of the spirit, or the spirit thinks of her." Similarly, the threat in *The Loss of Virginity* seems to come both from within, through the girl's willingness to expose herself, and from without, through the threatening animal, and, of course, through the title. As for the condition of virginity itself, Gauguin understands it to be brought into question merely by the nakedness of the girl in *Manao tupapau*, but his commentary deliberately leaves the question in suspense: "it is a slightly indecent study of a nude, and yet I wish to make of it a chaste picture."

Beginning with Jean de Rotonchamp, who was outspokenly unsympathetic to what he viewed as the literary pretensions of the picture, interpreters of *The Loss of Virginity* have exploited the notion of symbolism to reduce the difference of title and image in favor of the meaning declared by the title. Thus, the animal is interpreted as a fox, "symbol of perversity"; the figures in the background as a wedding procession, "normal denouement" to the loss of virginity; and the plucked flower as a symbol of vanity, evidence that the girl has already submitted to desire, even if she remains physically virgin at the moment depicted in the painting.[20] This last reading is offered despite the critic's observation that Gauguin has substituted an iris for the conventional lily, symbol of purity, and that Gauguin later distinguished his work from that of Puvis de Chavannes on the basis of his avoidance of such conventional symbolism, so readily yoked to the service "of comparison with former ideas and with other authors."[21] Such "understanding" was not the response Gauguin sought, he protested: "Puvis would call a painting 'Purity,' and to explain it he would paint a young virgin holding a lily in her hand—a familiar symbol; consequently one understands it. Gauguin, for the title 'Purity,' would paint a landscape with limpid waters; no stain of the civilized human being, perhaps a figure"—a Tahitian figure, no doubt, since by the time he wrote these words Gauguin had left "civilized human beings" behind and moved to Tahiti.

Though it is sometimes taken for one of Gauguin's Tahitian paintings, *The Loss of Virginity* is set in Brittany, the nearest "primitive" locale to which Gauguin had access while he was still living in France.[22] The Tahitian spirit of the painting overall suggests that the loss signified by the title may be concentrated in the "stain of the civilized human being" introduced by the wedding procession, who would thus figure not merely the denouement, but the *cause* of the loss, by reenacting the scene of Susanna and the Elders, which Gauguin held to be impossible in Tahiti.[23] Seeing the girl and animal as a center of purity certainly conforms with Williams's reading, which seems intent on reversing the symbolic meanings proposed by Gauguin's critics. The fox, for instance, is domesticated to a "hound," and it is "watchful" in a protective rather than a threatening sense. However, its principal function in Williams's reading is to signal that the girl is otherwise "unattended." Williams emphasizes that the girl is "nude," or even "naked," and that she lies "in an open field," from which Williams has erased even the iris, the sheaf of grain, and the tufts of grass that Gauguin particularized, and that we might have expected Williams to treat with the loving attention he so often paid to such detail. In this case, apparently, nothing, not even nature itself, is to be allowed to interfere with the sense of openness, which Williams seems to associate with innocence.

Recognizing this association, one can also recognize what has become of the threat posed by the wedding procession, whom Williams does not mention explicitly. They have been translated into the structure of Williams's poem, threatening the openness of innocence with a closure that Williams identifies with the title. The stanzas referring to the title frame those referring to the painting, thus:

```
┌──── STANZA 1 (TITLE) ────┐
│                          │
│       STANZA 2           │
│      (PAINTING)          │
│                          │
│       STANZA 3           │
│      (PAINTING)          │
│                          │
└──── STANZA 4 (TITLE) ────┘
```

As Brueghel had done with his Virgin, in a way that Williams interpreted as threatening, Williams has placed Gauguin's virgin "among the words." But the threat of closure is perpetually deferred in the displacement between the title of Gauguin's painting and that of Williams's poem. Williams's title closes upon itself—the title is "The Title"—at the same time that it opens out in reference to Gauguin's painting. Similarly, the title serves to frame the poem, as an external element, at the same time that it takes up an internal position, within the poem's syntax, as its first line.

Williams departs, then, from conventional interpretation of Gauguin, not by denying the existence of symbolism but by recognizing a spatial factor in the relation between symbols. This recognition is encouraged by the spatial nature of Gauguin's art, but it corresponds to the function of "spacing" in the literary art of Gauguin's symbolist colleague, Mallarmé, as analyzed by Jacques Derrida in "The Double Session." Like Williams, Mallarmé was interested in the visual qualities of the printed text, such as the white space that conventionally distinguishes the "body" of a text from the title that stands at its "head." To Mallarmé, the whiteness of that space betokened virginity, but beyond such symbolism, its semiotic blankness protected the purity of the text against contamination by reference to anything beyond itself, including the reference signified by the title.[24]

The white space thus marks the "unrelatedness" of text and title remarked in Williams's poem, and the text in its purity is virginal, "unattended," like the girl in Gauguin's painting. But just as Williams refers to the attendance of the "watchful hound" to establish the "unattended" condition of the girl, some relation to the title is needed to establish the "unrelatedness" of the text. The white space is thus a place simultaneously of disrelation and of relation. It withdraws from signifying activity even as it makes that activity possible. Marking the "unrelatedness" of the title, in Williams's terms, it "enhances the impact / and emotional dignity of the whole." In the terms Derrida derives from Mallarmé, it is "the spacing that guarantees both the gap and the contact" (261), the "hymen" that signifies both separateness (virginity) and fusion (marriage) (209–16). Referring to an effect like the one Williams achieves through his play with the title of his poem, Derrida observes that, "*inserting* a sort of spacing into interiority . . . no longer allows the inside to close upon itself or be identified with itself" (234).

Such self-identity would be a form of self-possession, as Derrida illustrates by quoting Jean-Pierre Richard's celebration of that condition as he believes Mallarmé to have constituted it: "Each self possesses itself in an other it nonetheless knows to be only another self" (271). Spacing prevents such identification, permitting instead the skewed "identity" of "the virgin and the whore" that Williams celebrates (*P* 210, 237). The whoredom consists in the lack of self-possession, but not in the presence of the opposite state, possession by another; the absence of that state constitutes virginity. Meaning always passes through the white space of the text, but never settles on it. Like *pharmakon, supplément, différance,* the terms from which Derrida extracts "a double, contradictory, undecidable value," Williams's virgin-whore "escape[s] philosophical mastery" (221), that is, possession by interpretation.

The interpreter, however, cannot escape his desire for such possession, according to Derrida (230). He—the masculine pronoun continues to be appropriate for this image of the interpreter—is possessed by his desire, and in submitting to that possession, he submits to the same spacing that operates within the text, for between his desire and its unpossessable object there is always a gap. This extension of the condition of textuality to the condition of the reader enables Derrida to say that the reader is read by the text (224). He is possessed by it, as he is possessed by desire. Such "violence inflicted on the reader" Derrida aligns with Nietzsche's discussion of a woman's power "to captivate us."[25] In Joseph Riddel's deconstructionist reading of Williams, an image of such capture is found in the Unicorn Tapestries treated in *Paterson* 5, where "the maimed unicorn, neutralized and captured, a King-self now interred in his own texts," has been lured there by the elusive presence of a virgin (*Glyph* 228, 222).

Before I consider an alternative reading of this medieval tapestry, another example of Williams's reading of modern painting will demonstrate that Williams reserves a place for the reader, or viewer, that is not merely engulfed in the folds of the text, or the painting, as the deconstructionists conclude. "A Matisse" (1921; *SE* 30–31), the essay or, perhaps, prose poem Williams wrote in response to seeing the *Blue Nude* (1907; fig. 20) in a New York gallery, extends the example of Williams on Gauguin in a number of ways.[26] Since "A Matisse" was written thirty-five years before "The Title," the essay provides another opportunity for exploring the persistence throughout Williams's career of the concerns central to my study. The most immediate of these, the problem of the Virgin, on which "The Title" focuses, is clearly set in the context of the problem of representation, in "A Matisse," by the addition of both the artist and the viewer to the list of dramatis personae. Finally, "A Matisse" can promote an understanding of the place of abstraction within the problem of representation, for Matisse is a direct heir to the mode of abstraction initiated by Gauguin, though the *Blue Nude* was also inspired by an earlier source, "the abstraction / of Arabic art," as Williams called it.[27]

The most ambitious analysis of "A Matisse" has been conducted by Charles Altieri, in the course of a passionately sustained and philosophically knowledgeable effort to counter the theory of textual indeterminacy identified with Derrida. Another work by Williams, the poem "This Is Just to Say" (1934), occupies a more central place in Altieri's argument than does "A Matisse" and establishes a context for the latter work that resembles the biographical context established in the opening section of this chapter. "This Is Just to Say" is another poem in which Williams asks his wife for forgiveness, although only for the seemingly insignificant offense of eating some plums that she had probably been saving for breakfast (*CP1*: 372). The reason for asking forgiveness is less important to Altieri than the implied conditions on which Williams, as Altieri understands him, expects the forgiveness to be granted. Altieri calls these conditions the "shared features of a life," but he would probably accept the term I have used, "marriage," in view of his explicit analogy "between the note's auditor (who, in a literary context is probably best seen as a wife) and a poetic audience" (*AQ* 168).

That some readers who make up the poetic audience will be approaching this poem, or even the work of this author, for the first time, means that the analogy between reader and wife cannot rest on the specific prior understandings we would assume to have been achieved between husband and wife. For Altieri, the poem itself evokes—he would say "performs"—the shared conditions through which its meaning can be determined. At the same time, the poem must eschew the temptation to offer commentary on its own performance, because that would introduce the vagaries of rhetoric exploited by deconstructionists to undermine the determinacy of meaning. "Forgiveness is only possible," Altieri concludes, "if one refuses to name it as his right and refrains from supplementing acts by explanations. *Just sayings* are not just sayings but doings" (*AQ* 174).

This purity of performance, the avoidance of explanation, is the lesson that Altieri feels modern writers learned from experiments in abstraction in the visual arts, and specifically, the lesson that Williams "performs" (*Dada* 110) in his response to Matisse's *Blue Nude*. "The skill of the artist who renders 'just' paintings, just because they are only paintings, not interpretations," finds its equivalent, within the painting, in "the immediacy of presence—the girl's satisfied nakedness" (*Dada* 112), and outside the painting, in Williams's prose, which is "the equivalent of Matisse's modernist distortion in the service of disclosure and direct rendering" (*Dada* 111). The image on the canvas is an abstraction in that it does not "represent" a woman so much as it "stages" the artist's state of mind, a claim that finds support, though Altieri does not appeal to it, in the fact that Matisse apparently did not use a life model when he painted the *Blue Nude*.[28] Similarly, Williams's essay does not "represent" the finished picture. It imagines the process that produced the picture. That the scene of production is imagined to include a life model need not embarrass Altieri, for a fictional setting can provide the scene for real action, the mental action that Williams shares with Matisse.

Such sharing is the equivalent of the "shared features of a life" that unite speaker and auditor in Altieri's account of "This Is Just to Say," but his account of modernist painting reveals more clearly the violence that establishes such community. The artist brings to bear "a counterpressure of lucidity and violence," or more simply, a "violent lucidity," against any tendencies that threaten the unity of a composition, whether it be the self, a work of art, or a society (*Dada* 116). In Picasso's *Demoiselles d'Avignon* (1907), for instance, which Altieri discusses following his analysis of "A Matisse," "the angularity and deformation at once insist on the threatening, castrating qualities of the women and the power of the artist to express and contemplate the dangers inherent in sexuality."[29] The threat of castration, from the male perspective that Altieri has adopted, is the ultimate threat to wholeness. Hearing that threat in the term "partiality" that Williams employs in his essay "Against the Weather" (1939; *SE* 199; cf. *AQ* 170), Altieri celebrates the opposing term, "identity," which "conquers 'partiality,' " in Altieri's reading (*AQ* 175). Such a reading overlooks Williams's stipulation that a relation between parts should be established "without destruction of their particular characteristics." The resulting "identity" is to be discovered "in their disparateness," like the "identity" of virgin and whore in *Paterson* 5.

For all his effort to formulate an alternative to deconstruction, Altieri does not escape the aesthetic of capture whose operation I have already suggested in Joseph Riddel's reading of Williams's unicorn theme. In Altieri's account of "A Matisse," Williams "captures a condition of authorial action" (*Dada* 111). In *Les Demoiselles*, Picasso is able "to capture the full threat women impose" (*Dada* 116), the threat being imposed, in this case, by a rival sex rather than a rival artist. One cannot help noticing that the marriage on which Altieri models his reading of "This Is Just to Say" is similarly based upon capture, despite Altieri's insistence that such admirable qualities as "self-knowledge and concern for another" are those which the author is able "to capture and make us reflect upon" (AQ 168). Although for Altieri the captor is the author (or the reader as author), while for Riddel it is the text, the two positions merely reflect each other in the hall of mirrors that leads from Hegel's concept of desire as the movement of self-consciousness. In particular, Hegel's analysis of the encounter between two consciousnesses as the struggle between master and slave informs Altieri's understanding of art as much as it does those theories that seem more openly to welcome interpretive violence.[30]

Against such theories, Julia Kristeva's analysis of love stands out as a more genuine alternative than Altieri's version of capture. To explain how she understands love, Kristeva explicitly distinguishes it from desire, as that concept has been elaborated, with ample acknowledgment to Hegel, in the psychoanalytic theory of Jacques Lacan.[31] A corollary to Kristeva's distinction of love and desire is the discovery of a form of identification that is not a mode of aggression, as it is in Lacan's theory of "captation by the image" and in Altieri's theory of reading that "captures a condition of authorial action."[32] In the case of Williams, only Kristeva's form of identification helps to explain the strange combination of intimacy and distance in the relation between "reader" and "text" in "A Matisse": "In the french sun, on the french grass in a room on Fifth Ave., a french girl lies and smiles at the sun without seeing us." Here is another woman who fascinates Williams by turning her eyes elsewhere.

At the most explicit level, the problem that Williams explores in "A Matisse" is the problem of the "local," to which Williams and Robert McAlmon had devoted the journal Contact, where Williams's essay first appeared. In his "Comment" in the same issue, by invoking the legend of St. Francis's communion with the animals, Williams announced his hope that there might be a common language that would permit communication among different localities without erasing their difference. "A Matisse" picks up that theme, distinguishing two localities in "the french grass" and "a room on Fifth Ave.," but it abandons the image of language. That "there was nothing to be told" is, Williams declares, a precondition of Matisse's painting.

For Altieri, that precondition promises freedom from rhetorical "displacement," ensuring "the power of art to capture, preserve, transmit, and elicit immediacy" and hence permitting the "transference" of that power, without "displacement," from France to America, from Matisse to Williams (*Dada* 111–12). However, by insisting, in the concluding words of his essay, that the "french girl lies and smiles at the sun without seeing us," Williams clearly indicates that whatever sense of immediacy the girl embodies is one to which "we" will gain access only through mediation. That function is performed by the figure of the artist, who is not pictured on the canvas but whose presence Williams infers from the quality of the light, or more precisely, from the luminosity of the color: "The sun had entered his [the artist's] head in the color of sprays of flaming palm leaves."[33] Thus identifying the artist with the sun, Williams can write that the girl "gave herself to them both." She is not captured; she gives herself, as Williams imagined that Mary would "give herself to her lover" (*P* 229). In each case, her willingness to give herself to another provides the basis for the relationship between the woman and an interested observer: Joseph, in the case of Mary; or Williams, in the case of the *Blue Nude*. From the perspective of the observer, the formula for the relationship is, "If she could love him, she could also love me" (cf. *TL* 34).

Unlike the more conventional schema of identification between two parties implied in Altieri's schema of capture, the triangular schema of primary identification proposed by Kristeva permits acknowledgment of the complex displacements at work in Williams's reading of Matisse without allowing those displacements to remove the possibility of determining a place for the reader, as deconstruction threatens to do. In the terms that Kristeva herself employs to mark her difference from deconstruction, she does not "give up on the subject" (*RPL* 142). Moreover, in her concern with placing the subject, she elaborates a theory of representation as the representation of place, which can take us one step further toward understanding what it means to say that the Virgin stands for Williams at the edge of representation.[34]

In "Motherhood According to Giovanni Bellini," Kristeva distinguishes between two modes of representation, one devoted to "reproducing bodies and spaces as graspable, masterable *objects*," the other pursuing a goal that is ultimately "objectless" (*DL* 246, 248), or in other words, abstract. Bellini portrays the figure of the Madonna as a graspable object, but his evocation of space, in Kristeva's view, inclines toward the other mode of representation, and ultimately toward an ungraspable "maternal space," made all the more inaccessible by special circumstances of Bellini's childhood (*DL* 247). If the mother is the infant's first object, Kristeva reasons, she must first be a nonobject, the space where objects first come into being (cf. *TL* 26, 36). That process is initiated by identification not merely with the mother but, more specifically, with her jouissance, her vision of an object of desire. Henceforth, the infant will see its objects in the light of that vision, but the mother's object, on which the vision was originally fixed, remains inconceivable, except as the source of light. It can only appear as "a blinding, nonrepresentable power—sun or ghost" (*TL* 36).

In equating the sun with the artist to whom the Blue Nude gives herself, Williams looks to the same evidence that leads Kristeva to deduce such a presence in Bellini: the chromatic luminosity of the painting itself, in excess of any figurative requirement but directed toward the "objectless goal" of "dazzling light" (*DL* 248). According to Kristeva, "the object-oriented ostentation of his time" (*DL* 266) discouraged such abstraction in Bellini and eliminated it from the art that followed him. "It reappears," Kristeva notes, "only in the work of certain modern painters (Rothko, Matisse) who rediscovered the technique of eclipsing a figure in order to have color produce volume" (*DL* 250). Chromatic volume, "luminous space" (*DL* 250), a space without figuration yet bounded by figures, like the blank space in "The Title"—this is the space in which Williams locates the figure of the Virgin. Her ambiguous status as virgin-whore is played out in the relation between the figure and the space.

Tracing the cult of the Virgin to its origins in the Eastern Church, Kristeva associates the importance of space in Bellini's paintings with the Greek definition of the Virgin as *ergasterion*, literally, a workshop, a place of production, which Kristeva generalizes as "privileged *space*" (*DL* 251, 264). Its analogy in the West would be the *hortus conclusus*, the image of the Virgin as an enclosed garden, which art historians see represented in the Unicorn Tapestries in the enclosures that contain the unicorn.[35] If the imageless space in Bellini is analogous to that in the tapestries, the images that "float," as Kristeva has it (DL 249), within or upon that space might also be analogous. The unicorn, then, would be equated with Bellini's figure of the Virgin. This equation finds support in medieval tradition, which posits a special affinity, by way of shared qualities, between the unicorn and the virgin who subdues it. However, the tradition also introduces a complication by identifying the virgin with Mary and the unicorn with Christ, whose desire for Mary, however virginal it might be, entraps him in the flesh through incarnation. Williams and his interpreters bring the motif of desire into greater prominence, in part by reading the unicorn's horn as a phallic emblem.[36] Rather than preventing the unicorn from representing the Virgin, however, such a reading reinforces Kristeva's distinction between two modes of representation.

According to Kristeva, the figure of the Virgin in Bellini's paintings, as opposed to the nonfigural space, results from the artist's desire to possess the virgin as a "graspable, masterable object" (*DL* 246), a desire that Kristeva understands to be phallic. "Is not the object-oriented libido always masculine?" she asks (*DL* 264). The Virgin's escape from such desire can only leave its nonobjective trace in the quality of the painting's space. If the combined image of the unicorn within the *hortus conclusus* describes a relation of capture, therefore, it is not simply a matter of equating capture with enclosure. At the start of *Paterson* 5, the initial sighting of the unicorn, "calling / for its own murder" (*P* 208), foreshadows the outcome of the hunt: the unicorn captures itself. The artist's desire to capture his object produces an image not of the object but of the desire. His failure to capture the object, meanwhile, opens an objectless space that acquires meaning through that failure, much as the white space opens beneath the title of "The Title," as the latter element circles around in endless self-pursuit.

Although his language does not always make it clear, the logic that Joseph Riddel employs carries him this far in his analysis of the unicorn theme in *Paterson* 5. At the far reaches of deconstructive irony, Riddel's word "capture" indicates the outflanking of the desire-to-capture by its ever-elusive object. Closure is perpetually deferred in that undecidable border region, neither outside nor inside, explored by Williams in "The Title," surveyed by Derrida in his study of Mallarmé, and claimed by Riddel in his study of Williams (*Glyph* 231 n8). For Derrida and Riddel, however, this field of indeterminacy is itself sealed within the endless limits of desire. Because desire is defined as the pursuit of that which is always already lost, the failure of desire is not its end, but rather its perpetuation. For the artist, or his opposite number, the reader, deconstruction provides no place outside desire, and therefore, strictly speaking, provides no place, because the notion of place requires a distinction between a "there" and a "here," a place for the object, and a place for the subject.[37]

Williams, on the other hand, repeatedly encounters something like an end to desire, "A / world lost," which "beckons to new places," as he wrote in the section of *Paterson* 2 published separately as "The

Descent" (*P* 77–79; *CP2*: 245–46). The "new places" are created by a distinction between a "there" and a "here," as between "the french grass" and "a room on Fifth Ave." in "A Matisse." Consequently, when Williams observes the occupant of that other place, the woman who figures the object of his desire, she need not take up the full range of his attention, any more than the Blue Nude fully absorbs Matisse. "She had chosen the place to rest and he had painted her resting, with interest in the place she had chosen," Williams explains. The place emerges when the figure of desire "lies down to rest a while," as Williams describes the unicorn in its enclosure (*P* 235). The enclosure, therefore, must be taken to mark not quite an end to desire, but a pause.

"There is no end / to desire," writes Williams in "Perpetuum Mobile: The City" (1936; *CP1*: 432), but there is the dream in which desire and love are "fused / in the night" (*CP1*: 430), the "dream of love" from which Williams's play of a decade later was to take its name. In lines from "Perpetuum Mobile" that Doc Thurber quotes repeatedly in the play, the dream is represented as a glow on the night horizon, the lights of a distant, unapproachable city, "All white!" (*CP1*: 430; cf. *ML* 122, 191, 193). Like the "pure luminosity" that Kristeva finds in Bellini (*DL* 268), the whiteness that Williams evokes throughout his work stands on a horizon, at the limit of signification. Nevertheless, it always signifies, even when, as in "The Title," it is no more than the white space between title and text. In "The Descent," it is "the memory / of whiteness" rather than plain absence, "whiteness (lost)." In *Paterson* 5, it is the married man's persistent image of the virgin whom he has whored, whose emblem is the "milk-white" unicorn (*P* 234).

 7. The Ethics of Painting

THE BLANK SPACE or whiteness to which one is led while following Williams in pursuit of the Virgin poses a challenge to any form of interpretation. It is the figure for the idea that Williams states thematically in the observation, "there was nothing to be told," in "A Matisse," or in the admonition, "be mostly silent," in "The Wanderer" and "Thinking Back Toward Christmas." It paradoxically presents for interpretation an object that is turned away from the interpreter, like Brueghel's Virgin with her "downcast eyes." If, in the poem that contains that phrase, Williams appears to identify the Virgin "as a work of art / for profound worship," it may seem that the only posture available to the interpreter confronted with such an object is one of subjection. Yet in the passage in *Paterson* 5 that treats the same painting, Joseph's relation to the Virgin seems very different from the adoration of the Wise Men, just as in "Asphodel," Williams seeks forgiveness from a position very different from the supplicatory pose he adopts in "For Eleanor and Bill Monahan." In "Asphodel," addressing his wife rather than the "Mother of God," Williams declares,

> I do not come to you
> abjectly
> with confessions of my faults,
> I have confessed,
> all of them.
> In the name of love
> I come proudly
> as to an equal
> to be forgiven.   (*CP2*: 326)

The position of equality assumed here may seem an alternative to subjection, yet the two positions intertwine so closely in Williams's work that they are better viewed as correlatives rather than alternatives.

Many readers, attracted to the position of equality assumed in "Asphodel," will want to argue that it depends on the very condition that I seem to deny when I insist that the object of interpretation, Virgin, wife, or text, is turned away from the interpreter, Joseph, husband, or reader. According to the counterargument, the attention of the listener, the poet's wife in the case of "Asphodel," is presumed in the fact that the poet addresses her. Though we do not hear her response in the words of the poem, that, too, is presumed in the speaker's anticipation of forgiveness. In other words, the poem implies a dialogue. As a model for the relationship between reader and text, the concept of dialogue has attracted an increasing number of critics in their search for an alternative to the bleak prospects offered by deconstruction. Most important for my purposes, dialogue promises to offer an alternative to the interpretive violence that deconstruction takes to be inevitable. Thus, in an exchange with Jacques Derrida, Hans-Georg Gadamer prefers the "good will" presumed of partners in dialogue to the "will-to-power" under which Nietzsche and his contemporary followers subsume the act of interpretation.[1]

A hermeneutic position such as Gadamer's faces a potentially fatal weakness, however, in that it must presume about the partners in the supposed dialogue so much that is not evident in the text or transcript of the dialogue itself. In the case of the lines I have quoted from "Asphodel," for instance, how do we know that the speaker is motivated by "good will" and not by what Jacques Derrida, in his response to Gadamer, calls "good-will-to-power"? In a discussion of his *Livre du dialogue*, the French poet Edmond Jabès has noted, "If I speak, I impose a certain silence on you. That's my power."[2] How does Jabès know that "he who is silent . . . wants to hear the word as it exists in itself in order to judge it in the best way possible"? On the other hand, if I put myself in the place of that silent judge, in the place of the interpreter, how do I know that the other whom I judge wants to submit to my interpretation, wants, that is, to be understood, or, in the case of a text, even to speak?[3] Contrary evidence is available in numerous statements by modern artists, of which Williams's "there was nothing to be told" is only one example. Instructed by such examples, critics have discovered similar resistance in more traditional works of art, as Williams seems to have discovered it in Brueghel.[4]

The comparisons I have drawn in the preceding chapters between Williams's practice and the theory of Julia Kristeva imply a third model of interpretation that differs from either the hermeneutic or the deconstructive models at significant points. It can be called "psychoanalytic," as long as that term is taken primarily to designate a mode of discourse, and one does not become mired in the muddier ontological questions of psychoanalytic theory, the "existence" of the unconscious, of the death drive, and so on.[5] Both Gadamer and Derrida situate psychoanalysis within the question of communication, the question that most radically separates their two positions. Gadamer would exclude psychoanalysis from his theory of hermeneutics because communication, on which Gadamer's theory depends, transmits what a speaker wants to say, whereas psychoanalysis sets out to interpret what a speaker does not want to say.[6] On the other hand, Derrida, skeptical of the possibility of communication, seeks to demonstrate that psychoanalysis, like Gadamer's hermeneutics, depends on that possibility. According to Derrida, the goal of psychoanalysis is the moment "when the analyst would say to the patient 'you' in such a way that there would be no possible misunderstanding on the subject of this 'you,' " that is, the pronoun would function as a proper name.[7] However, "if the most secret proper name has its effect of a proper name only by risking contamination and detour within a system of relations," as Derrida claims to demonstrate, "then it follows that pure address is impossible. I can never be sure when someone says to me—or to you—says to me, 'you, you,' that it might not be just any old 'you.' "

Locating psychoanalysis midway between the positions adopted by Gadamer and Derrida, Kristeva accepts the deconstructive critique of communication but at the same time holds onto the possibility of "amorous dialogue . . . not as communication but as *incantation*. Song dialogue."[8] *Tales of Love* makes clear that such dialogue has a basis very different from the Platonic model that Gadamer invokes. Characterizing Platonic dialogue as "a struggle of discourse," Kristeva goes on to characterize the deconstructive critique of Platonism as only another form of power play, replacing the violence of dialectic with the violence of rhetoric (*TL* 67–68). In contrast to both positions, she offers the promise of "relaxation of consciousness, daydream, language that is neither dialectical nor rhetorical, but peace or eclipse: nirvana, intoxication, and silence" (*TL* 81). The promise is based on a fantasy, "the loving dialogue of the pregnant mother with the fruit, barely distinct from her, that she shelters in her womb," but the fantasy is repeatedly enacted, in Kristeva's experience, in the privileged space of the psychoanalytic session. It is an essential stage in the dialogue of the patient with "the (loving) silence of the analyst" (*TL* 1), who does not "say to the patient 'you,' " as Derrida would have it, but rather permits the patient to say "I."

By an analogous refusal to address but nevertheless to engage its audience, "the text turns out to be the analyst and every reader the analysand," as Kristeva states (*RPL* 210), and psychoanalytic method provides the basis for a theory of interpretation. Kristeva's analysis serves two interrelated objectives that I have pursued throughout this study. First, the view of interpretation that Kristeva elaborates holds out the possibility of resisting the temptation of violence, which I might call my theoretical objective. Second, application of Kristeva's practice permits a reading of Williams that I believe to be demonstrably less violent than that produced by the reigning alternative modes of interpretation: hermeneutics and deconstruction. Having sketched out the theoretical difference by locating Kristeva between Gadamer and Derrida, I will turn now to the practical question by returning to Williams's *Spring and All*. From there, the theoretical question posed by Williams's choice of painting as text will lead us, finally, back to Williams's reading of Brueghel. By this time, it should not be surprising to find that every attempt at applying a theory of reading to Williams turns into a reading of theory. In Williams's texts, theory and practice are inseparable.

Spring and All opens by acknowledging the problem with which I opened this chapter, the problem of the orientation of a work of art toward its audience. "To whom then am I addressed?" Williams asks (*CP1*: 178). The issue has grown especially problematic after Williams's decision, just before posing this question, that "my fellow creature . . . doesn't exist," because he—or she, Williams takes care to add—is blocked by outmoded forms from the experience of the present moment, the only moment in which true existence is possible. In the absence of fellow creatures, but in the presence of himself, whose existence he senses "in a bastardly sort of way," Williams decides that he is addressed "to the imagination." As soon as he has established that orientation, however, he immediately turns to address the reader directly for the first time: "I myself invite you to read and to see." There follow the images of the "fraternal embrace, the classic caress of author and reader," discussed above in chapter 5.

This passage poses the relation to the reader in two forms, engagement and disengagement, both of which retain their full force within the framework of dialogue as Kristeva conceives it. The "fraternal embrace" of author and reader is a mode of identification, but as such, it is not simply a fusion. It is made possible by the fact that the author is turned away from the reader toward a Third Party, here called the imagination. The reader identifies not with the author but with his address to the imagination. Though the difference of author and reader will prevent the latter from ever knowing exactly what was said in the author's address, the reader can participate in the activity of saying. He cannot see the imagination from the author's position, but in response to the author's invitation "to read and to see," the reader learns that he, too, can have a position, an "I" that is both a word to speak and an eye from which to see.

In contrast to this reading, both deconstruction and hermeneutics must erase one of the forms of relation between author and reader that Williams posits. Hillis Miller, approaching by way of deconstruction, emphasizes the total alienation from the reader represented in Williams's claim that the reader does not exist. That claim is only intensified in the image of the "fraternal embrace," in which, according to Miller, "Williams' readers must abandon their separate selves and lose themselves in the imagination of the poet" (*Daedalus* 421; *LM* 373). Miller projects an aggressive tone onto Williams's seemingly innocent image by reading back from a later thought-experiment—ultimately a failure, as both Williams and Miller concede—in which Williams imagines "the annihilation of every human creature on the face of the earth" (*CP1:* 179), in the hope of providing for a new beginning.

From a position opposite to Miller's, Thomas Whitaker does less violence to the tone of the "fraternal embrace" passage by reading it as an image of "dialogue," but because he understands that term more in Gadamer's sense than in Kristeva's, Whitaker, in his turn, must erase the difference between author and reader that provides Williams with his starting point.[9] Rather than situating the imagination, as Kristeva would do, as an unrepresentable "elsewhere" toward which author and reader orient themselves from their separate positions, Whitaker conceives of the imagination as a place within which author and reader dwell in common understanding.[10] The violence required to establish such understanding, however, resonates in Gadamer's characterization of the hermeneutic project as a matter "of alienness and its conquest."[11] One is reminded of Charles Altieri's campaign for "an 'identity' that conquers 'partiality' " (*AQ* 175).

A resistance to hermeneutic conquest gathers in Williams's work particularly around those points that are most indebted to painting. According to Gadamer, texts "always express a whole," but "dumb monuments" of visual art, because of the physical medium that commits them to "finiteness and transience," leave understanding "curiously unsure and fragmentary."[12] Because, like Gadamer, Whitaker wants the poem to be an act, always open to our response, he regrets the numerous statements in which, often by analogy to painting, Williams conceives of "the poem as an object, as a thing."[13] The very notion of an object places it "out there," beyond the magic circle of the imagination that Whitaker reserves for dialogue.

Nevertheless, Whitaker frequently alludes to one of Williams's analogies to painting, the notion of "conversation as design" derived from the art of Juan Gris as Williams considers it in his experimental prose work *A Novelette*.[14] Like so many other formulations by Williams, including the complex relationship with the reader established at the opening of *Spring and All*, the notion of "conversation as design" combines two elements that it is difficult to hold in balance. The term that Whitaker wants, of course, is "conversation," and he accuses others of distorting Williams's meaning by abstracting "design" from the life of conversation.[15] For his own part, however, Whitaker may be accused of permitting conversation to absorb design so thoroughly that the latter term retains no trace of its original reference to the visual arts. An attempt to restore that reference can benefit from Whitaker's warning against abstracting design but still draw a useful distinction between Williams's sense of conversation and Whitaker's.

The view that Whitaker wants to oppose, because it reduces "design" to an abstract, formal principle, is oriented toward Juan Gris's theoretical writings, which some evidence indicates Williams read (*I* 286, *SE* 132, *SL* 130). For both Rob Fure and Henry Sayre, for instance, a key point of correspondence between Williams and Gris is the phrase "formal necessity," employed by Williams in his *Autobiography* (*A* 264), and by Gris in his essay "On the Possibilities of Painting" (1924), which declares, "It is a question of fitting this rather shapeless world into these formal necessities."[16] The version of the essay Williams is thought to have read, however, was in French and was published twenty-five years before Williams wrote his *Autobiography*. Thus, the argument that Williams subscribed to a formalist aesthetic, or did so for part of his career, requires confirmation in Williams's own writing, apart from whatever he may be presumed to have read in Gris. Sayre attempts to offer such confirmation when he interprets Williams's design in the light of other terms from *A Novelette*: the "singleness" that Williams associates with Gris, and something called "the simplicity of disorder" (*I* 287, 275). Taking "singleness" and "simplicity" to denote unity, Sayre concludes, "the revelation of an abstract design unifies the disorder and multiplicity of the world" (*VT* 31). In fact, however, rather than advocating unity, *A Novelette* explicitly locates the "excellence" of writing in "the disjointing process" (*I* 285). The "singleness" and "simplicity" that Williams praises are not the qualities of a whole but rather of individual things; they are synonyms for "separateness."

The separateness of things in the art of Juan Gris seems to have made a deeper impression on Williams than either the moral or aesthetic unity over which Whitaker and the formalists argue. In *Spring and All*, Williams interrupts his prose discussion of Gris with two poems, elsewhere titled "The Rose" and "At the Faucet of June," which emphasize edges as a matter both of theme—"each petal ends in / an edge" ("The Rose")—and of form:

> the son
>
> leaving off the g
> of sunlight and grass ("At the Faucet of June")[17]

By calling attention to the words themselves—for instance, the way the word "song" contains the word "son"—Williams participates in "the modern trend" that he identifies with Gris: "the attempt . . . to separate things of the imagination from life" (*CP1*: 194). To accomplish this separation, the artist permits things to remain "recognizable" (*CP1*: 197), as they are in life, but alters the relation among the things and between the things and the viewer. It is the same process that Williams ascribes to Brueghel,

> who painted
> what he saw—
> many times no doubt
> among his own kids but not of course
> in this setting

In *A Novelette*, once again with Gris in mind, Williams illustrates how an imaginative "setting" or "design" functions as "conversation," in the special sense in which he employs that term.[18] "To be conversation," Williams advises, "it must have only the effect of itself, not on him to whom it has a special meaning but as a dog or a store window" (*I* 287)—two examples that Williams seems to have chosen precisely for their unrelatedness. Gris furnishes another such pair of examples, as Williams continues: "It must have no other purpose than the roundness and the color and the repetition of grapes in a bunch, such grapes as those of Juan Gris which are related more to a ship at sea than to the human tongue" (*I* 287). As objects in a painting, a bunch of grapes and a ship at sea might bear some relation to each other. In *Spring and All* (*CP1*: 197–98), for instance, Williams describes the combination of "a bunch of grapes" and "sea and mountains" in Gris's *The Open Window* (1921; fig. 22). In relation to the viewer, however, such objects are to be considered from afar, like a ship at sea, not consumed, like a bunch of real grapes.

To advance his view of dialogue, Whitaker compensates for the tendency toward separateness in Williams's "conversation as design" by situating that notion in the context of marriage, a traditional emblem of communion. *A Novelette* is the work in which Williams poses the relation between writing and marriage that I noted at the end of chapter 5, and much of the text consists of "marital conversation," as Whitaker calls it, between Williams and his wife.[19] However, rather than creating a picture of communion, Williams's examples of marital conversation prove to be just as disjointed as the rest of the text:

> When writing is not witty it is dull.
> Take a guitar.
> Nonsense.
> Really, I wish I could believe that. (*I* 287)

At one stage, pressed by the demands of his patients during a flu epidemic, by his wife's demands for ordinary attention from her husband, and by the demands he makes on himself in his desire to write, Williams warns, "I must pare my life to the point of silence—though I hope surliness may never intervene—in order to get to the paper" (*I* 280).

Paper inscribed at the point of silence bears a strong resemblance to canvas marked with paint, but if each medium closes off the possibility of one type of conversation, it opens up the possibility of another type, in which one of the partners is turned away, like Mary in Brueghel's Epiphany scene, or like Williams himself in *A Novelette*. In that text, in addition to comparing writing to marriage, Williams also compares writing to "unrelated passing on the street," but he insists that such a conception can "rescue us for a design that alone affords conversation" (*I* 287). In *Paterson* 5, after the "woman in our town" has passed him in the street and disappeared, Williams's persona addresses her in her absence, saying, "have you read anything that I have written? / It is all for you" (*P* 220).

The logic of such a claim requires, first, an identification of words as things such as Whitaker denies, and second, the recognition in such an identification of an ethical dimension, whose apparent absence may be the chief reason for Whitaker's denial of the first condition. Williams's essay on "French Painting," which names Juan Gris as an example (*RI* 71), clearly reveals the basis of the identification of words as things in the analogy between writing and painting: "Stein has stressed, as Braque did paint, words" (*RI* 70). After making that claim, Williams offers the illustration of Gertrude Stein's famous motto, "A rose is a rose—which printed in a circle," thereby supporting the analogy with visual art, "means two things," Williams explains: "A rose is, to be sure, a rose. But on the other hand the words: A rose is—are"—the plural verb now suiting the number of words—"words which stand for all words and are very definitely not roses." Williams concludes: "In this case the words are put there to represent words, the rose spoken of being left to be a rose."[20] Thus, all of Williams's writing can be *for* the "woman in our town" precisely in the sense that it is not addressed *to* her but rather to the words themselves. When the words are permitted to be themselves, rather than set in pursuit of a referent, the woman, who might have been the referent, is permitted to be herself.[21] Williams draws the same lesson explicitly from Gris in *A Novelette*: "Singly he says that the actual is the drawing of the face" (*I* 286); the drawing is drawing, it is not a face. "And so," Williams continues, "the face borrowing of the drawing—by lack of copying and lack of a burden to the story—is real."[22] What the face borrows of the drawing is chiefly "the quality of independent existence," as Williams describes it in *Spring and All* (*CP1*: 207–8).

It seems easy enough to recognize an ethical dimension in the result of this logical sequence, which reaffirms the ancient rule of respect for persons. What has hindered such recognition is the origin of the sequence, not in respect for persons but in respect for things. The entanglement of ethics in a traditional notion of the human subject makes the move from "conversation as design" to "marital conversation" essential for Whitaker to maintain a "moral correlative of the artistic act."[23] In contrast, deconstruction's critique of humanism has suggested the possibility of reformulating the basis for ethics. Hillis Miller has pursued such a formulation in connection with Williams's treatment of words as things.

Again, comparison of Whitaker's and Miller's reading of *Spring and All* will help to clarify their disagreement. Just as in *A Novelette* Williams asserts that "to be conversation, it must have only the effect of itself," so in *Spring and All* he insists, "the word must be put down for itself, not as a symbol of nature but a part, cognizant of the whole—aware—civilized" (*CP1*: 189). To deemphasize Williams's treatment of words as things, Whitaker puts as much weight as possible on the "personification" implied in words such as "cognizant" and "aware," which he takes to be signs of human agency, supporting his view that words are acts.[24] On the other hand, Miller, who regrets any tendency to personification as a contamination of the linguistic purity of Williams's work (*LM* 387), places all of his emphasis on the need to put down the word for itself, which he regards as an "ethical obligation to the words or in the words" (*LM* 385). Extended from the writer to the reader, this obligation becomes the basis for what Miller calls "the ethics of reading" (*LM* 354).

Despite its role in distinguishing the two positions, "the word itself" is finally subordinated in Miller's ethics as well as in Whitaker's. A hint of this subordination can be detected in the phrase I have just quoted from *The Linguistic Moment*, where Miller vacillates in his assignment of the ethical obligation "to the words or in the words." In his book entitled *The Ethics of Reading*, Miller concludes decisively that the source of that obligation may be in the words, but it is not the words themselves. "The endpoint of my exploration of the ethics of reading," he declares, "is the strange and difficult notion that reading is subject not to the text as its law, but to the law to which the text is subject" (*ER* 120). Miller identifies this law with the "matter" or "thing" that the text is about (*ER* 118), but his use of the word "thing" in this sense serves Miller mainly as a springboard to the more problematic concept of "the thing" in the philosophies of Heidegger and Derrida (*ER* 103–5). From that context, Miller derives a paradoxical notion of the "thing" as something essentially nameless that nevertheless commands an effort to name it. That command is the law to which the text, and ultimately the reader, is subject. Since its paradoxical nature precludes the possibility of fulfillment, obedience to the law necessarily involves violation, abuse or violence. Hence, "violence is the human and transhuman law," Miller proclaims (*LM* 336).

These mysteries are helpfully dramatized in the example that provides the climax of *The Ethics of Reading*. Miller considers an image in Henry James's preface to *The Golden Bowl*, in which James likens his experience of rereading his earlier works to the experience of walking across "a shining expanse of snow spread over a plain," in which someone else has already left tracks.[25] In James's analogy, those earlier tracks are the words of the text written by his earlier self. As he reads those words now, he finds that his present gait no longer fits their pattern; he cannot walk in the tracks that are already there but occasionally must make new impressions on the snow. Rather than complaining of discomfort, however, James reports a sense of exhilaration comparable to "a sudden large apprehension of the Absolute."[26] That apprehension, figuratively, is of the snow itself, which James identifies with "the clear matter" that the original text sought to cover. James can welcome the difference between the terms of the original texts and the terms that now come to him, and which become the text of his prefaces, because, Miller infers, his obligation is not to any text but to that "clear matter" that he takes as his law. He can come to know that law only through difference, the difference of the two texts from each other signaling the difference of the "matter" from any text that attempts to approach it.

Miller's interpretation of James's image of the snow-covered plain runs parallel, up to a point, with my interpretation of Williams's image of the Virgin. In both cases the failure of representation draws attention to a blank or white space marking representation's limit. In fact, in the chapter on Williams in *The Linguistic Moment*, Miller employs one of Williams's essays on Marianne Moore (1925) to much the same ends that James's preface serves in *The Ethics of Reading*. The Moore essay provides a full measure of the operation by which Miller simultaneously asserts and denies the privilege enjoyed by "the word itself" in Williams's poetics, for Miller's chapter begins by quoting the essay as an assertion of that privilege: "Miss Moore gets great pleasure," Williams writes, "from wiping soiled words or cutting them clean out, removing the aureoles that have been pasted about them or taking them bodily from greasy contexts" (*SE* 128; *LM* 352–53). The question of what might be done with words after they have received this treatment leads Williams to the figure that Miller quotes at the end of his chapter. The words can be arranged in a "design," Williams says, as "white circular discs grouped closely edge to edge upon a dark table make black six-pointed stars" (*SE* 129; *LM* 386; fig. 23). One perceives the black stars in between the discs, as James perceived the "shining expanse of snow" in between the various impressions left on it. Both perceptions are of something luminous, although that quality, only hinted in the shape of Williams's stars, emerges more clearly elsewhere in the essay on Moore, where the ground is figured as white rather than black: "this white light that is the background of all good work" (*SE* 122).

Moore's words arranged as white discs form an image of the "conversation as design" proclaimed by Williams in *A Novelette*, the title piece of the collection in which Williams first reprinted the Moore essay. But the emergence of the design in negative space permits Miller to employ it as an image of the "ethics of reading," and as an occasion for turning away from the words themselves. "The starry design is not the words themselves," Miller argues, "but the black space between them shaped by the words or brought by them into a kind of negative visibility" (*LM* 386). Of course, because Williams's image is spatial, the black space is no less visible than the white discs that surround it, though it may be, as the perceptual psychologists tell us, that we cannot see both as a pattern at the same time.[27] Miller's argument relies on introducing time into Williams's spatial image, ultimately converting a visual experience into a linguistic one.

In itself, this does not differ radically from Williams's procedure, which is, after all, an attempt to illustrate something about words. But where Williams seems to have chosen a visual analogy in order to stress what visual and linguistic experience have in common, Miller's reading of the analogy stresses an essential difference. "Why must we represent to ourselves in spatial terms what is not spatial but verbal and temporal?" Miller asks, summarizing one of the main themes of *The Linguistic Moment*. "Why," he continues, "must this topographical structure always fail in the encounter with something that cannot be spatially located, that has no *topos* and no proper name?" (*LM* 338). For Miller, the black space in Williams's image stands for that nonspace, and its relation to the discs is a "troping as turning away, naming by not naming" (*LM* 387).

The trope that names the nameless is catachresis, the term that I borrowed from Miller in chapter 2 to represent the deconstructive aspect of Williams's reading of the Baby in Brueghel's Epiphany scene. I concluded that chapter by suggesting that catachresis does not necessarily involve for Williams the violence that deconstruction discovers in it. Now that we have explored Williams's treatment of the other figures in the Epiphany scene, we can understand his alternative to violence in terms of the story that those figures tell. If troping, as in Miller's definition, is a "turning away," the Epiphany scene presented by Brueghel offers a dramatic analogue by suggesting that Mary has turned away from Joseph. I have argued that Williams accepts the commonly understood meaning of that turn, that Mary has taken a lover, but he does not accept its common valuation. Reading from Joseph's position, Williams interprets Mary's turning away from him not as an abuse of their relationship but rather as a renewal of it. Such a reading operates on assumptions that differ radically from those that most critics of *Paterson* 5 share with Miller. His valuation of sexual promiscuity as violence or abuse colors his valuation of the rhetorical trope.

As Miller presents this connection, the rhetorical problem comes first and serves to explain why, for instance, "adulterous liaisons form the obscure (or not so obscure) background of most of James' fiction" (*ER* 106). Novels such as James's "promise an ultimate bringing of the moral law into the open" (*ER* 33), but in fact they manage only to present a figure of that law, as if in negative space. Accordingly, "they impose on the reader the experience of a betrayal like that of being betrayed by his or her beloved." In fact, this experience turns out to be a complicated network of reciprocal betrayals. If the text betrays the reader, devotion to the law "forces the reader to betray the text" (*ER* 120), in the act of "misreading" for which deconstruction has become notorious. Moreover, as Miller seeks to demonstrate in his study of James's preface to *The Golden Bowl*, the reader might never have been aware of the law if the text had not first betrayed it. "It could be said," Miller generalizes, "that any text falsifies or mistranslates the 'thing.' It is unfaithful to the thing by being what it is, just these words on the page" (*ER* 121).

While this statement may seem to contradict Williams's rule that "the word must be put down for itself," in fact it reveals the context in which Miller understands that rule to operate. Words put down for themselves are "just these words on the page," but the command that they must be put down does not come from the words but from the "thing" that the words are set to translate. The linguistic law that renders "translation . . . both necessary and impossible," a favorite theme of deconstruction, is the force that drives the endless cycle of betrayal in Miller's ethics of reading, because it involves words in the seemingly hopeless task of bridging the gap between the universal and the particular.[28] Hegel's statement of the problem remains, for once, its most succinct formulation: "What I only mean or suppose is mine: it belongs to me—this particular individual. But language expresses nothing but universality; and so I cannot say what I merely *mean*."[29] In Derrida's terms, proper names, words put down for themselves, in their particularity, continually undergo a process of conversion to common nouns. This is, for instance, the process that prevents the psychoanalyst, according to Derrida, from finding a particular "you" to designate the analysand in the supposedly climactic moment of therapy.

My claim that Williams and Kristeva offer an ethics of reading that does not necessitate betrayal rests on the assumption that they regard the relation of the universal and the particular from a different perspective than that adopted by deconstruction. At times, Kristeva seems to be recommending that the universal be bypassed altogether in favor of an ecstatic, if illusory, uniqueness. "Being in love," the condition that Kristeva takes as her model of discourse, "conveys a throbbing, passionate, unique meaning, but only here and now, and which might, in another juncture, be absurd" (*TL* 276). Williams seeks a compromise by insisting that concentration on the "here and now" leads to discovery of "the universality of the local." In "Against the Weather" (1939), he glosses that phrase by describing a mode of communication with others that does not destroy their separateness: "From me where I stand to them where they stand in their here and now—where I cannot be—I do in spite of that arrive! through their work which complements my own, each sensually local" (*SE* 198).

Despite their differences, these statements by Williams and Kristeva share two points that distinguish them in crucial ways from the deconstructive propositions I have been considering. In the first place, Kristeva's emphasis on the "throbbing, passionate" quality of meaning and Williams's insistence on the "sensually local" assume the force of "the body itself speaking," as Williams once called it (*Int* 98). This force is conspicuously absent in Derrida or Miller, even when they use sexual analogies. In the second place, and perhaps as a consequence, the exchange that Kristeva and Williams are describing is not a process of translation, which would be "absurd," according to Kristeva. The artist "does not translate the sensuality of his materials into symbols but deals with them directly," Williams declares (*SE* 197). Rather than translation, Kristeva, following Freud, proposes the psychoanalytic transference as an analogue for the dynamics of love.[30] Williams, too, describes a transference, the conveyance not merely of meaning, as in translation, but also of the subject, "from me where I stand to them where they stand."

Although Williams recognized that his notion of "the body itself speaking" might be linked to psychoanalytic concepts, "to the ritualistic, amoral past of the race, to fetish, to dream" (*Int* 97), the example of Cézanne rather than Freud seems to have first suggested to Williams the possibility of "a meaning without saying anything at all" (*Int* 53), and painting, rather than psychoanalysis, is the ground on which the division between Williams and Derrida appears most clearly. Geoffrey Hartman has noted that Derrida tends to discuss painting in a "deflected form." Even when a painter is his immediate subject, as in his essay on Valerio Adami, Derrida "still evades the problem of the painterly moment," Hartman suggests, "in favor of the penetration of the graphic into picturemaking."[31] In other words, Derrida considers painting as a form of writing. This deflection has important consequences for "the materiality of the signifier," which I introduced in chapter 3 as an issue that brings Derrida and Williams together. As in the case of catachresis, they come together only to disagree.

Derrida's materiality might best be understood as the particularity that stands on one side of the deconstructive abyss, over against universality. In "Freud and the Scene of Writing," for instance, "the materiality of the signifier" is associated with an "idiomatic residue" that defies translation.[32] This residue is in no way "perceptual," however, as it is for Freud. In contrast to Williams's notion of the "sensually local," Derrida's particularity rejects physical embodiment. Although some proponents of deconstruction lay claim to a "sensible language," Derrida announces "happily" that the graphic play involved in his famous concept of *différance* is permitted only if we "refer to an order which no longer belongs to sensibility."[33] When *différance* is generated from *différence* by the substitution of one letter, "the difference marked in the 'differ( )nce' between the *e* and the *a* eludes both vision and hearing," Derrida contends. It eludes hearing because the two words are given the same pronunciation. It eludes vision, however, only because Derrida chooses to dismiss the visual nature of his example as an accident of representation, though an inescapable one. Like Miller in his reading of Williams's image of words as white discs, Derrida interprets a visible difference as only a "negative visibility."

A similar deflection is at work in Miller's response to Williams's analogies between writing and painting. Though Miller accepts such analogies as inevitable, he resists them with the kind of moral fervor that he enjoins on the reader in relation to the law of the text. As if the mixture of arts were adulterous, Miller seeks to preserve their difference.[34] Unlike painting, he argues, writing involves "the naming power of words" or the "power of referring to something beyond itself," which opens the abyss between the particular and the universal (*PR* 305; *LM* 378). This argument takes into account Williams's insistence on the role of representation in writing, but it does not take into account his claim that all painting, too, is representational, or better, "conversational," a term that reflects Juan Gris's example of "conversation as design."

From Gris's example Williams learned that painting can be no more purely "for itself" than writing can be. Both media establish a relationship to something "beyond." But painting's lesson to writing is that "naming" or "referring," to adopt Miller's terms, are not the only modes for establishing that relationship. It can also be established through the materiality of the medium, perceived not as mere matter but as "matter to stir the sensual depths in men," in the phrase from Matisse that Kristeva applies to Giotto (*DL* 221). Such stirring results in the process that I have called transference, following Kristeva's distinction of transference and reference (*TL* 273–77). Only by assuming such a process could Williams have extended his concept of "conversation as design" to,

> Pollock's blobs of paint squeezed out
> with design!
> pure from the tube. (*P* 213)

The "simplicity of design" that Williams discovered in Marianne Moore is comparable (*SE* 129). Although "unlike the painters the poet has not resorted to distortions or the abstract in form" (*SE* 123), she is like the painters in her attitude toward her materials. She is like Brueghel, whose eye for material has an effect that Williams equates with the fine quality of "stuff" from which the suits of his peasants were woven (*P* 228). "There is a 'special' place which poems, as all works of art, must occupy," Williams acknowledges in his essay on Moore, "but it is quite definitely the same as that where bricks or colored threads are handled" (*SE* 125). Because she handles each word "in such a way that it will remain scrupulously itself, clean perfect" (*SE* 128), as if it were "squeezed out pure from the tube," Moore is also like Pollock. Through such handling, Moore serves "the 'thing' which is her concern" (*SE* 130), as much as it was Henry James's. But as Williams reads Moore, "this 'thing' [can] grow clearer, remain fresh, be more present to the mind" (*SE* 126), because it is revealed to the senses at the edges of words that are treated as things. It does not withdraw into "an order which no longer belongs to sensibility," as happens in deconstruction's obsession with naming the nameless.

"The word . . . experienced as word and not as a simple substitute for a named object," in Roman Jakobson's formula, provides the basis for "the ethics of linguistics" proposed by Julia Kristeva (*DL* 31). If Derrida tends to remove the materiality from "the materiality of the signifier," Kristeva tends to remove the signifer, arguing that the poet wants to provide language "with its matter independently of the sign." While Williams would avoid both extremes, there is nevertheless sufficient agreement between Kristeva and Williams on the issue of materiality to permit extrapolation from Kristeva's "ethics of linguistics" to an "ethics of reading" that would accord with Williams's practice more closely than Miller's version.[35]

Kristeva's analysis of "The Song of Songs" in *Tales of Love* provides a useful focus for such extrapolation. In addition, since "The Song of Songs," as Kristeva emphasizes (*TL* 99–100), can be read as the address of a female speaker to a male beloved, it provides a further safeguard against misunderstanding my previous concentration on an example in which a male observer, Joseph, regards a female beloved, Mary. As I have already suggested in other connections, I do not want to imply any "natural" correlation between male and female genders and the positions of subject and object. Nor would I want to maintain an oppressive association between women and certain of the attributes that I have attached to Mary, for instance, silence and materiality. My purpose has been, rather, to explore a dynamic relationship in which identities, including those of gender, are not fixed, and in which neither silence nor matter deserve the connotations of passivity that traditionally attach to them. One of the lessons that Williams derived from painting, as I have noted, is that matter generates meaning "without saying anything at all."

Within the "amorous dialogue" of the "Song of Songs," Kristeva distinguishes two "motions" (*TL* 93–94). The first is a motion of idealization, the conception of the beloved as "supreme authority" (*TL* 90). Its relevance to an ethics of reading is brought out elsewhere, when Kristeva refers to it as the fantasy of "One Meaning" or "unique meaning" (*KR* 310, 314; *DL* 224; *TL* 276). From the lover's perspective, of course, it is more than a fantasy, obtaining not merely "here and now" but universally. Kristeva will go thus far toward acknowledging the universal that Miller apprehends as the "thing" or "law," and that Williams briefly glimpses as "His rule," looming beyond the figure of the Virgin in "For Eleanor and Bill Monahan" (*CP2*: 254). Williams's example confirms the insight that Kristeva derives from psychoanalysis, that such perception repeats a founding encounter with a double object, the "father of individual prehistory" sensed through the mother, in her orientation away from the infant perceiver. A gap thus threatens between the perceiver, lover, or reader, on the one hand, and, on the other hand, the law, which appears to be inaccessible. The initial response to that gap is, for Kristeva as for Miller, a sense of "subjection" (*TL* 94). This is the posture that Miller assumes when he reads poems by Williams, such as "Young Sycamore" or "Spring and All," "as if the words . . . , proferred one by one, were each an invocation. Each word is different, but each asks for the same hidden otherness, the 'radiant gist,' to appear," though that request is bound to go unanswered (*LM* 389).

Kristeva reads the "Song of Songs" as an "invocation" (*TL* 88, 92, 93), but in a very different sense from the one that Miller attributes to Williams. Not only this difference, but the entire difference between Kristeva's ethics of reading and Miller's, depends on the second "motion" of amorous dialogue, to which nothing in Miller's ethics corresponds. It is a motion of identification, but it is not simply a leap over the gap that separates the lover and her ideal. Rather, the lover discovers something in the gap with which she can identify both the beloved and herself. That something is the material of signification, which comes to substitute for the absent body of the beloved. The erotic charge that the lover would invest in that body is instead invested in the body of signs, a metaphoric operation that Kristeva designates as transference, in accordance with the etymological meaning of the word "metaphor," "*metapherein* = to transport."[36] Simultaneously, another transference takes place, which accords more closely with the psychoanalytic meaning of that term. The lover transfers herself to the body of signs by becoming their subject, or in plainer language, she joins herself to speech by speaking. In this way, "supreme authority . . . can be loved as flesh while remaining essentially inaccessible" (*TL* 90), as Kristeva points the paradox. The body of the beloved remains absent, but his "flesh" is present in the words that the lover uses to invoke him. This invocation does not imply only absence, as it does for Miller. Kristeva's lover speaks not to, but in the absence of the beloved.

It is possible to draw out the implications of Kristeva's schema for an ethics of reading by summarizing its two "motions" as follows: out of the experience of "subjection" to One Meaning, or law, the "subject" thus constituted, whether as reader or lover, experiences the potential of many meanings. In "reader-response" theory, a comparable experience often leads to an elevation of the reader over the text, "the reverse" of the relation that Miller advocates (*ER* 10). In contrast to either of these positions, Kristeva envisions, paradoxically, the sharing of "supreme authority." The speaker in the "Song of Songs" "sets herself up as equal, in her legal, named, unguilty love, to the other's sovereignty," Kristeva concludes (*TL* 99). The legality of this relationship assumes a continued faithfulness to the other, a condition of married love, as Kristeva stresses (*TL* 96–97), rather than the infidelity from which Miller's ethics cannot escape. On the other hand, the equality of the relationship depends on a challenge to the status of the other as the seat of One Meaning. The reader does not claim that meaning "belongs to me," as Hegel does, for instance, in the statement I quoted earlier. Nor can she even claim that the many meanings have a single source. Either of these alternatives would simply place the seat of One Meaning in a different location. Nevertheless, the possibility of many meanings first emerges with the introduction of a single additional figure into the marital relation, and that introduction may appear to threaten infidelity.

In performing the second motion of Kristeva's schema, the speaker of the "Song of Songs" does, in a way, take a lover. Perhaps sensing this dimension of the poem, Ernest Renan, as Kristeva notes, postulated the existence of a third character in the drama, a shepherd, to whom the speaker gives her love in the king's absence (*TL* 89–90). For Kristeva, this third character is a representative of the king, or the law, and a representative not merely in name but in body. It is the body of signs, or in terms of our allegory of reading, the text, to which the speaker transfers her initial attachment to the king's body. In terms of Kristeva's psychoanalytic theory, the ultimate source of any subsequent bodily sensation would be the speaker's "own" body, but she would experience that body neither as her own nor as a unity

(*RPL* 27, 101). Her experience is rather one of "heterogeneity," which is relived through the text. As Kristeva defines it, the text is radically other, having "no addressee," and its pretense to unity is "pulverized."[37] However, against Miller's claim that "the text is not the law nor even the utterance of the law but an example of the productive force of the law" (*ER* 121), Kristeva permits the claim that the text is the utterance of the law because productive force has been transferred to the text in its materiality. Thus, the relation of the text to the law is not a betrayal, in Miller's sense of misrepresentation. Nor does the reader, in order to be faithful to the law, need to betray the text by misreading it.

Only a practice very different from reading as it is ordinarily conceived, however, can permit the reader to sense the bond between the text and the law. Confronted with texts such as Joyce's, Kristeva finds that, "*reading* means giving up the lexical, syntactic, and semantic operation of deciphering, and instead retracing the path of their [the texts'] production" (*RPL* 103). Williams had the same author in mind when he wrote, "by his manner of putting down the words it is discovered that he is following some unapparent sequence quite apart from the usual syntactical one" (*SE* 28). *Spring and All* elaborates on the "manner of putting down the words" that Joyce's practice illustrated: "the word must be put down for itself." And Williams's essay on Marianne Moore returns to the difficulty of reading words thus put down: "They forget, those who would read Miss Moore aright, that white circular discs grouped closely edge to edge upon a dark table make black six-pointed stars" (*SE* 129). If this is a definition of reading, one might well ask, with Kristeva, "how many readers can do this?" (*RPL* 103). The exemplar will not be found in "the established critic," who "will not read," Williams complained (*SE* 121).

As Kristeva's work on the problem of interpretation has evolved, she has placed increasing emphasis on the psychoanalyst as exemplary reader, notably in her essay "Psychoanalysis and the Polis" (1981; *KR* 301–20). This perspective requires a significant enlargement of the model I earlier cited from Kristeva, in which the reader corresponds to the analysand, and the text, in its silence, corresponds to the analyst (*RPL* 210). The more complete model acknowledges that the analyst is not merely silent but also works to construct an interpretation. Moreover, both interpretations, that of analyst and that of analysand, are driven by desire, which is always involved in the desire to know, Kristeva insists (*KR* 308). Accordingly, both interpretations will move toward an imagined object of desire, the illusion of One Meaning, conceived in a process that Kristeva compares with delirium and that corresponds to the first "motion," that of idealization, in her analysis of the "Song of Songs."

The second "motion" is peculiarly the work of the analyst, who is distinguished from the analysand by the former's recognition of the role of desire in interpretation. That recognition permits the continual reimmersion of any fixed meaning in the fluid process from which it arose. As Kristeva explains, "if I know that my desire can make me delirious in my interpretive constructions, my return to this delirium allows me to dissolve its meaning, to displace by one or more notches the quest for meaning which I suppose to be *one* and *one only* but which I can *only* indefinitely approach" (*KR* 310). Within this configuration, the silence of the analyst performs two functions. On the one hand, it brings out the desire in the analysand's interpretation by permitting it to operate as freely as possible, through the mechanism of transference. On the other hand, it also exposes a countertransference. The analyst can hear the desire at work in his or her own interpretation, as that interpretation is suspended in silence.

Williams protested against early attempts to apply psychoanalytic categories to literature (*SE* 85–90), yet in his own poetic practice he evolved a method of interpretation that is remarkably similar to the psychoanalytic method I have just described. The first book of *Paterson* (1946) poses the problem of interpretation through the image of the falls:

> The water pouring still
> from the edge of the rocks, filling
> his ears with its sound, hard to interpret.   (*P* 17)

This sound becomes meaningful only indirectly, as it is heard in the silences of a dialogue that could be either of love or of therapy:

> We sit and talk
> quietly, with long lapses of silence
> and I am aware of the stream
> that has no language, coursing
> beneath the quiet heaven of
> your eyes   (*P* 24)

In the image of "the quiet heaven" can be seen the ideal object constructed by the lover's desire. But in those "long lapses of silence,"

the lover is able to acknowledge what was previously "unacknowl-
edged desire" (*P* 25), as he hears "the stream / that has no language,"

> which has no speech; to
> go to bed with you, to pass beyond
> the moment of meeting, while the
> currents float still in mid-air, to
> fall   (*P* 24)

As the current of desire, the stream is for Williams, as for Kristeva
(e.g., *TL* 92, 99), a "violent torrent" (*P* 24), but the image of "the
quiet heaven" floats upon it, like Kristeva's "loving discourse . . .
afloat on primal repression" (*TL* 84).

In response to the question, raised at the beginning of this chapter,
as to whether the interpreter is to adopt a posture of subjection to or
equality with the text, the model suggested by the psychoanalyst's
practice as Kristeva presents it indicates that both postures are neces-
sary. An ideal meaning must be postulated in order to stimulate the
process of making meanings, but all meanings must be recognized as
provisional, good "only here and now," if the process is not to stop.
Like Kristeva, Williams calls that process the "imagination."[38] Neither
would separate the work of imagination and interpretation as they
have traditionally been divided between the creative artist and the
critic or analyst. However, when he examined the work of interpreta-
tion, Williams's own work as an artist naturally led him to draw his
examples from artistic rather than psychoanalytic practice. Among
Williams's examples, that of the painter Brueghel stands out promi-
nently. Williams's ideas about interpretation had begun to gather
around the figure of Brueghel as early as the drafts for *Paterson* 2
(1948):

> What is the river saying below the falls
> strewn with exposed rocks, emaciated—what
> to the eyes, the nose?
>
> What to Breugel? What to anyone. Is it
> saying nothing —?[39]

In *Paterson* 5 Williams employs Brueghel's *Adoration* to demonstrate
that a text that appears to be "saying nothing" might nevertheless
speak "to the eyes, the nose," after the manner in which the falls speak
in *Paterson* 1.

The Virgin of Brueghel's *Adoration* promises the quiet heaven of her eyes, but by keeping them "downcast," as Williams specifies in "Pictures from Brueghel," she keeps their meaning inaccessible. In the silence that thus gapes, the stream of desire can be heard in the murmurs of the Soldiers. However, those murmurs are not heard by the Wise Men, who remain in subjection to the Virgin, but rather by Joseph, who enjoys a relation of equality with his wife by acknowledging his distance from her. Joseph thus sees, within the painting, the "two sides" from which Brueghel produced the painting, in Williams's concluding assessment:

> Peter Brueghel the artist saw it
> from the two sides: the
> imagination must be served—
> and he served
> > dispassionately

There are two sides to the imagination served by Brueghel, or addressed by Williams in *Spring and All*. One side is an ideal of order. The other side is a "process of ordering," in which "order is broken down to be redistributed."[40]

To acknowledge the utopian quality that attaches to the side of the ideal in such a scheme of interpretation, but at the same time to emphasize the mobility ensured by the attraction of the other side, Kristeva refers to the analyst's constant shifting between desire and neutrality as a "polytopia" (*KR* 306, 311, 319). Many modern observers have responded to a utopian dimension in Brueghel. Claude Lévi-Strauss, for instance, associated the enchantment of the Brazilian rain forest with "those pictures by the Brueghels in which Paradise is marked by a tender intimacy between plants, beasts and men."[41] Surely Williams had such a picture in mind when he imagined the harmonious existence of the American Indians "as a natural part of a beloved condition" (*IAG* 138) or the pastoral communion between St. Francis and the beasts, blessed with a vision of One Meaning.

But it was equally important for Williams that that vision be dissolved and the communicants released to go their separate ways. When the artist, following the example of St. Francis, unites us in a "common language," nothing prevents our "retaining our devotional character of Wolf, Sheep, and Bear" (*SE* 29). Similarly, the "riotously gay rabble" in Brueghel's *The Wedding Dance* (ca.1566; fig. 24), though,

> Disciplined by the artist
> to go round
> & round,   (*CP2*: 390)

resist that centripetal force as they,

>   go openly
> toward the wood's
> edges

Whether the edges be of woods or of words, like "white circular discs grouped closely edge to edge," Williams keeps an eye on the space beyond.

Appendix

THE BRUEGHEL PASSAGE IN *PATERSON* 5
(*P* 226–28)

Peter Brueghel, the elder, painted
a Nativity, painted a Baby
new born!
among the words.
Armed men,
savagely armed men
armed with pikes,
halberds and swords
whispering men with averted faces
got to the heart
of the matter
as they talked to the potbellied
greybeard (center)
the butt of their comments,
looking askance, showing their
amazement at the scene,
features like the more stupid
German soldiers of the late
war

—but the Baby (as from an
illustrated catalogue
in colors) lies naked on his Mother's
knees
—it is a scene, authentic
enough, to be witnessed frequently
among the poor (I salute
the man Brueghel who painted
what he saw—
many times no doubt
among his own kids but not of course
in this setting)

The crowned and mitred heads
of the 3 men, one of them black,
who had come, obviously from afar
(highwaymen?)
by the rich robes
they had on—offered
to propitiate their gods

Their hands were loaded with gifts
—they had eyes for visions
in those days—and saw,
saw with their proper eyes,
these things
to the envy of the vulgar soldiery

He painted
the bustle of the scene,
the unkempt straggling
hair of the old man in the
middle, his sagging lips

——incredulous
that there was so much fuss
about such a simple thing as a baby
born to an old man
out of a girl and a pretty girl
at that

But the gifts! (works of art,
where could they have picked
them up or more properly
have stolen them?)
—how else to honor
an old man, or a woman?

—the soldiers' ragged clothes,
mouths open,
their knees and feet
broken from 30 years of
war, hard campaigns, their mouths

watering for the feast which
had been provided

Peter Brueghel the artist saw it
from the two sides: the
imagination must be served—
and he served
          dispassionately

 *Notes*

CHAPTER 1

1. Williams, "An Approach to the Poem," *English Institute Essays 1947* (New York: Columbia University Press, 1948), 51. I have corrected Williams's misspelling of Hartpence's name in this account. Other versions of the Hartpence anecdote appear in *A* 240 and *RI* 218.

2. On minimal art and sculpture, see Marcelin Pleynet, "Art minimal," *Art et littérature* (Paris: Seuil, 1977), 347–53.

3. As I explain in my concluding chapter, I would set the "ethics of painting" against the "ethics of reading" proposed by Hillis Miller (*ER*). Other recent titles of particular relevance are Tobin Siebers, *The Ethics of Criticism* (Ithaca, N.Y.: Cornell University Press, 1988); Mark Edmundson, "The Ethics of Deconstruction," *Michigan Quarterly Review* 27 (1988): 622–43; and Wayne C. Booth, *The Company We Keep: An Ethics of Fiction* (Berkeley and Los Angeles: University of California Press, 1988). The ne plus ultra of this trend in titles is represented in a series of three sessions on "The Ethics of Ethics" at the 1988 convention of the Modern Language Association. A historical series might be traced through Julia Kristeva's "The Ethics of Linguistics" (1974), in *DL* 23–35; Jacques Lacan's seminar of 1959–60, *L'Ethique de la psychanalyse* (Paris: Seuil, 1986); and Simone de Beauvoir's 1948 essay *The Ethics of Ambiguity*, trans. Bernard Frechtman (New York: Citadel, 1962). The alternatives available to artists at the end of World War II are posed most sharply by Jean-Paul Sartre, *What Is Literature?* trans. Bernard Frechtman (New York: Harper and Row, 1965), and Roland Barthes, *Writing Degree Zero*, trans. Annette Lavers and Colin Smith (New York: Farrar, Straus and Giroux, Noonday, 1968). As Susan Sontag points out in her preface to Barthes (xi), portions of that work began to appear in the same year, 1947, that saw publication of Sartre's book.

4. O'Hara, "Jackson Pollock," *Art Chronicles 1954–1966* (New York: Braziller, 1975), 18.

5. See Miller, *PR* 9, quoted in the next paragraph.

6. Foucault, "The Discourse on Language," *The Archaeology of Knowledge*, trans. A. M. Sheridan Smith (New York: Pantheon, 1972), 229; Derrida, *Of Grammatology*, trans. Gayatri Chakravorty Spivak (Baltimore: Johns Hopkins University Press, 1976), 127; both cited in Siebers, *Ethics of Criticism*, 227, 82.

7. On the grounds that "works of art stand . . . as metaphors for non-violence," Michael Phillipson proposes to construct "an ethics, a politics of criticism" (*Painting, Language, and Modernity* [London: Routledge and Kegan Paul, 1985], 92, 181). While sharing his aims, I differ considerably from Phillipson in method, especially from his uncritical embrace of deconstruction.

8. *PR* 9. Miller's reference is to the famous poem 22 of *Spring and All* (*CP*1: 224), published separately as "The Red Wheelbarrow."

9. Alpers, BFP. I adopt Williams's spelling of Brueghel's name.

10. Alpers (*BFP 165*) identifies the nineteenth-century view with René van Bastelaer and Georges Hulin de Loo, *Peter Bruegel l'Ancien: son oeuvre et son temps* (Brussels: van Oest, 1907).

11. Alpers, "Art History and Its Exclusions: The Example of Dutch Art," *Feminism and Art History: Questioning the Litany*, ed. Norma Broude and Mary D. Garrard (New York: Harper and Row, 1982), 187. This essay originated in a paper read at the Women's Caucus for Art session, "Questioning the Litany: Feminist Views of Art History," College Art Association Annual Meeting, New York, 1978.

12. Alpers, "Art History and Its Exclusions," 196. On Vermeer in this regard, cf. SK 168 and *AD* 222–24. At times, however, Alpers attributes to Vermeer a mode of relationship that is distinctly possessive, e.g., "Vermeer signed the map and paints the woman" (*AD* 168).

13. See chap. 7, note 36, for references to relevant passages in Kristeva.

14. See esp. "Motherhood According to Giovanni Bellini" in *DL* 237–70, and "Stabat Mater" in *TL* 234–63.

15. See appendix for the passage from *Paterson*; fig. 5 for Brueghel's painting. The details of Williams's description make it clear that he has in mind the London painting, rather than one of the two other Epiphany scenes attributed to Brueghel, in the Musées Royaux des Beaux Arts, Brussels (ca. 1557) and the Oskar Reinhart Collection, Winterthur (1567). For reproductions of these works, see Max J. Friedländer, *Pieter Bruegel*, trans. Heinz Norden, *Early Netherlandish Painting* 14 (New York: Praeger, 1976), nos. 2 and 39. Previous criticism of the Brueghel passage in *Paterson* 5 includes: Riddel, *IB* 291–92, and *Glyph* 225–26; Ulrich Bachteler, *Die Darstellung von Werken der Malerei in der amerikanischen Lyrik des 20. Jahrhunderts* (Frankfurt/Main: R. G. Fischer, 1979), 196–201; Mariani, *NWN* 708–9; Sayre, *VT* 122–23, 134–37; Christina Giorcelli, "William Carlos Williams' Painterly Poems: Two Pictures from a Bruegel," *Word & Image* 4 (1988): 200–208; Terence Diggory, "The Reader in Williams and Brueghel: *Paterson* 5 and *The Adoration of the Kings*," *Criticism* 30 (1988): 349–73.

16. See Paul de Man, *Allegories of Reading: Figural Language in Rousseau, Nietzsche, Rilke, and Proust* (New Haven, Conn.: Yale University Press, 1979), 204–6.

17. Riddel, *Glyph*. Riddel's earlier, book-length study of Williams also deals with the hunt in *Paterson* 5 (*IB* 274–88), but amid theoretical confusion that the later essay attempts to avoid, at least partly in response to Hillis Miller, "Deconstructing the Deconstructers," *Diacritics* 5.2 (1975): 24–31.

CHAPTER 2

1. In his note on "The Gift," *CP*2: 514, Christopher MacGowan rejects the frequent assertions linking Williams's poem to Giotto's *Adoration of the*

Magi in the Arena Chapel in Padua. Although the two works were paired in a Hallmark Christmas card issued in 1962, communications to me from both Webster Schott, director of the series in which the card was issued, and Linda Smith, the present design director at Hallmark Cards, confirm that Williams was not consulted in the choice of a visual work to accompany his poem. Other Christmas poems by Williams include "Gothic Candor" (1943); "Burning the Christmas Greens" (1944); "Thinking Back Toward Christmas: A Statement for the Virgin" (1944); "Christmas 1950"; "December" (1951); "For Eleanor and Bill Monahan" (1953); and "An Old-Fashioned German Christmas Card" (1959)—all now collected in *CP2*. Interestingly, the dates of the series make it contemporary with the evolution of *Paterson*. Before that period, however, the Christmas season had accumulated symbolic significance in Williams's life as the time of his first child's birth in 1914 and his father's death in 1918. See Mariani, *NWN* 111, 155–56; Terence Diggory, "New Contexts for Reading Williams: The Christmas Series," *William Carlos Williams Review* 16.1 (1990): 16–21.

2. James Joyce, *Stephen Hero* (New York: New Directions, 1963), 211, placed in cultural context in M. H. Abrams, *Natural Supernaturalism: Tradition and Revolution in Romantic Literature* (New York: Norton, 1973), 421–22.

3. For background, see Miller's review of Abrams's *Natural Supernaturalism*: "Tradition and Difference," *Diacritics* 2.4 (1972): 6–13.

4. Abrams, *Natural Supernaturalism*, 424. Cf. Northrop Frye on the ironic reversal of "the point of epiphany," especially in modern literature, in *Anatomy of Criticism: Four Essays* (Princeton, N.J.: Princeton University Press, 1971), 206, 223, 237.

5. For a deconstructionist critique of incarnation, see Jacques Derrida, *Glas*, trans. John P. Leavey, Jr. and Richard Rand (Lincoln: University of Nebraska Press, 1986), particularly 48a, for the link to symbolism, and 223a, for the dualist structure of opposition. In *Enlarging the Temple: New Directions in American Poetry during the 1960s* (Lewisburg, Penn.: Bucknell University Press, 1979), Charles Altieri acknowledges Miller's *Poets of Reality* as his starting point (26n2) but advances beyond that point partly by mounting an extended critique of incarnation as a doctrine of criticism (55ff). The phenomenological mode of that doctrine is applied to Williams by Cary Nelson, *The Incarnate Word: Literature as Verbal Space* (Urbana: University of Illinois Press, 1973), chap. 8.

6. Miller brought attention to the prose passages in *Spring and All* by reprinting selections, for the first time since the book's original publication, at the head of *Views*. See also *Daedalus*.

7. Kenneth Burke, "Heaven's First Law," reprinted in Miller, ed., *Views*, 47–48. Cf. Abrams, *Natural Supernaturalism*, chap. 7, on the Romantics' "extraordinary emphasis . . . on the eye and the object and the relation between them" (375).

8. *CP2*: 323. On the common origin of "Asphodel" and *Paterson* 5 in Williams's "River of Heaven" manuscript, see Sayre, *VT* 118. "Asphodel" took its final form in Williams's collection, *Journey to Love* (1955).

9. The skepticism implied by the whispering is discussed by Wolfgang Stechow, *Pieter Bruegel the Elder* (New York: Abrams, [1970]), 54.

10. Michel Foucault, *The Order of Things: An Archeology of the Human Sciences* (New York: Random House, Vintage, 1973), 133.

11 Cf. Samuel van Hoogstraten's characterization of the image produced by the camera obscura as "natural painting," noted by Alpers (SK 162).

12. *A* 359–62. Riddel (*Glyph* 204) and Miller (*LM* 388) comment on the passage. Recently, the notion of "presence" has featured prominently in Bernard Duffey, *A Poetry of Presence: The Writing of William Carlos Williams* (Madison: University of Wisconsin Press, 1986).

13. Derrida, *Spurs: Nietzsche's Styles*, trans. Barbara Harlow (Chicago: University of Chicago Press, 1979), 85.

14. Derrida, *The Truth in Painting*, trans. Geoff Bennington and Ian McLeod (Chicago: University of Chicago Press, 1987), 326.

15. Derrida, *Margins of Philosophy*, trans. Alan Bass (Chicago: University of Chicago Press, 1982), 247.

16. *Daedalus* 427. Miller's reference is to Aristotle's *Poetics* 1457b.

17. *CP1*: 235. Cf. Riddel *IB* 295–97; Miller *PR* 309; *Views* 11–13; *Daedalus* 425, 427; *LM* 379–80.

18. See Svetlana Alpers, "Describe or Narrate? A Problem in Realistic Representation," *New Literary History* 8 (1976): 27. For differing views of the effectiveness of color in Brueghel's London *Adoration*, cf. Gotthard Jedlicka, *Pieter Bruegel: Der Maler in seiner Zeit* (Erlenbach-Zurich: Rentsch, 1938), 252; and Stechow, *Bruegel*, 92. Adrian Stokes, *Colour and Form*, 2d ed. (London: Faber, 1950), chap. 5, makes Brueghel a prime example of a painter who captures through color a quality of "presentness," on which see David Carrier, "The Presentness of Painting: Adrian Stokes as Aesthetician," *Critical Inquiry* 12 (1986): 753–68.

19. Steiner, *The Colors of Rhetoric: Problems in the Relation between Modern Literature and Painting* (Chicago: University of Chicago Press, 1982), 114.

20. *SE* 27–29. A note to this reprinting incorrectly designates the source as *Contact* 1. I am grateful to Carl Rapp for drawing my attention to this passage.

21. See Marvin T. Herrick, "Catachresis," *Princeton Encyclopedia of Poetry and Poetics*, ed. Alex Preminger, enlarged ed. (Princeton, N.J.: Princeton University Press, 1974), 104.

22. Derrida, *Margins of Philosophy*, 255.

23. Paul Mariani ("The Hard Core of Beauty," in Mariani, *A Usable Past: Essays on Modern and Contemporary Poetry* [Amherst: University of Massachusetts Press, 1984], 85) tells of Kenneth Rexroth calling Williams "the most Franciscan poet he knew," a designation Mariani deems inapt. Glauco Cambon (*The Inclusive Flame: Studies in Modern American Poetry* [Bloomington: Indiana University Press, 1965], 185) and James Breslin (*William Carlos Williams: An American Artist* [New York: Oxford University Press, 1970], 205) refer to the presence of St. Francis in "The Mental Hospital Garden" (1954) to distinguish the gentleness of Williams's late work from the

tone of earlier work. I am skeptical of such periodization of Williams's career generally and certainly do not feel it can be gauged by the presence of St. Francis, who appears in Williams's work throughout his career. In addition to the early "Comment" in *Contact* and the late "Mental Hospital Garden," see, for example, *CP1*: 130, 414; *SE* 216; *RI* 166; *BU* 262–63; Mariani, *NWN* 335; Benjamin Sankey, *A Companion to William Carlos Williams'* Paterson (Berkeley and Los Angeles: University of California Press, 1971), 93; Charles Doyle, *William Carlos Williams and the American Poem* (New York: St. Martin's Press, 1982), 108.

CHAPTER 3

1. On Williams's ambivalence, see Dickran Tashjian, "Translating Surrealism: Williams' 'Midas Touch,' " *William Carlos Williams Newsletter* 4.2 (1978): 1–2.

2. *RI* 159, 166. This text presents in expanded form the essay first published in 1941 and reprinted in *SE* 241–49.

3. *CP1*: 131. These lines do not appear in the revised version of the poem (*CP1*: 414–15) that was printed in *The Collected Earlier Poems of William Carlos Williams* (1951).

4. Williams, "An Approach to the Poem," *English Institute Essays 1947* (New York: Columbia University Press, 1948), 69. The fullest treatment of this topic is Stephen Cushman, *William Carlos Williams and the Meanings of Measure* (New Haven, Conn.: Yale University Press, 1985).

5. On the theme of theft in Williams, see Reed Whittemore, *William Carlos Williams: Poet from Jersey* (Boston: Houghton Mifflin, 1975), chap. 4; on the theme in deconstruction, see Geoffrey Hartman, *Saving the Text: Literature/Derrida/Philosophy* (Baltimore: Johns Hopkins University Press, 1982), 91–95.

6. Derrida, *Margins of Philosophy*, 248. The reference is to *Metaphysics* 1006b.

7. The designation "highwaymen" alternates with "tradesman" (*sic*) in an early draft (Yale). The same draft shows the word "and" preceding the word "offered." The general direction of revision is toward the removal of connectives, "despised" by Marianne Moore, as Williams had observed (*SE* 124).

8. Christina Giorcelli ("William Carlos Williams' Painterly Poems: Two Pictures from a Bruegel," *Word & Image* 4 [1988]: 202) observes the absence of crowns. I am grateful also to Harry Gaugh for raising this question, and to Christopher Collins for questioning Williams's grammatical ambiguity.

9. Dvořák, *The History of Art as the History of Ideas*, trans. John Hardy (London: Routledge and Kegan Paul, 1984), 86.

10. For bibliography on this topic, see Hugo Kehrer, *Die heiligen drei Könige in Literatur und Kunst* (1908–9; reprint, Hildesheim: Olms, 1976), 1: 55n1.

11. Dvořák's essay on Brueghel, originally published in 1920, is quoted at length in Gustav Glück, *Peter Brueghel the Elder* (New York: Braziller, 1952),

one of the books that Florence Williams identified as her husband's sources for "Pictures from Brueghel" (*CP2*: 504).

12. Lawson-Peebles, "William Carlos Williams' *Pictures from Brueghel,*" *Word & Image* 2 (1986): 21.

13. Williams, "America, Whitman, and the Art of Poetry," *Poetry Journal* [8.1] (1917): 30.

14. Williams, "America, Whitman, and the Art of Poetry," 28.

15. *Williams' Poetry Talked About by Eli Siegel and William Carlos Williams Present and Talking: 1952* (New York: Terrain Gallery, 1964), 18. This pamphlet is included in the collection from Williams's library at Fairleigh Dickinson University, Rutherford, N.J.

16. In addition to "St. Francis Einstein of the Daffodils" and *VP*, Williams refers to Venus, for instance, in *CP1*: 6, 56; *SE* 125; *I* 282; *White Mule* (Norfolk, Conn.: New Directions, 1937), 1; *CP2*: 112, 184, 192, 394, 487; *P* 202; *A* 3.

17. A draft version makes the connection to Mary explicit (Yale; words italicized here are canceled in the manuscript):

> . no woman is virtuous
> who does not give hersel[f] to her lover,
> *as Mary did,* forthright .
> *or not at all*

18. See Michèle Richman, "Sex and Signs: The Language of French Feminist Criticism," *Language and Style* 13.4 (Fall 1980): 62–80. Richman's exposition is informed by a theory of gift economy deriving ultimately from Marcel Mauss's essay of 1925, *The Gift*, trans. Ian Cunnison (Glencoe, Ill.: Free Press, 1954), the context in which I would also set the following account of Williams's economics. For more by Williams on woman as gift, see *IAG* 183.

19. On Calas and alchemy, see Mike Weaver, *William Carlos Williams: The American Background* (Cambridge: Cambridge University Press, 1971), 145–56. In addition to their collaboration on the *Midas* project, Williams also translated poems by Calas. See Tashjian, "Translating Surrealism"; and *CP2*: 38–41, 451–52.

20. Ferdinand de Saussure, *Course in General Linguistics*, ed. Charles Bally and Albert Sechehaye, trans. Wade Baskin (New York: McGraw-Hill, 1966), 67–68; Derrida, *Of Grammatology*, trans. Gayatri Chakravorty Spivak (Baltimore: Johns Hopkins University Press, 1976), 47.

21. Derrida, "Structure, Sign, and Play in the Discourse of the Human Sciences," *Writing and Difference*, trans. Alan Bass (Chicago: University of Chicago Press, 1978), 289.

22. Many critics have agreed with Randall Jarrell in diagnosing Williams's economic theorizing as a regrettable infection that Williams caught from Pound. See Jarrell, ". . . *Paterson* Has Been Getting Rather Steadily Worse" (1951), in Charles Doyle, ed., *William Carlos Williams: The Critical Heritage* (London: Routledge and Kegan Paul, 1980), 239–40. Recent criticism, however, has placed greater emphasis on Williams's difference from Pound in

this area, and less emphasis on separating Williams's economics from his poetics. See esp. Kurt Heinzelman, *The Economics of the Imagination* (Amherst: University of Massachusetts Press, 1980), chap. 7; and Jay Rogoff, "Pound Foolishness in *Paterson*," *Journal of Modern Literature* 14 (1987): 35–44. Richard Sieburth ("In Pound We Trust: The Economy of Poetry/The Poetry of Economics," *Critical Inquiry* 14 [1987]: 152) is justified in claiming that "Pound's ideal form of economic exchange is direct barter." Pound's analysis of barter, however, tends to shift imperceptibly into an analysis of exchange by "tokens." See Pound, "A B C of Economics," *Selected Prose 1909–1965*, ed. William Cookson (New York: New Directions, 1973), 235.

23. Pound, "Gold and Work," *Selected Prose*, 347; cf. Sieburth, "In Pound We Trust," 154–55.

24. For Williams's "helium plus" in a Derridean context, see Riddel, *IB* 244. Cf. Derrida on the productivity of *différance*, *Margins of Philosophy*, 11.

25. For one instance of the common misreading, see Glauco Cambon, *The Inclusive Flame: Studies in Modern American Poetry* (Bloomington: Indiana University Press, 1965), 182–83. Cambon places the principle of "no ideas but in things" in the context of Pound's "imagism" and Williams's "objectivism," disregarding Williams's distinction of the latter from the former on grounds that he later associated with Brueghel. See Williams, "Objectivism," in Alex Preminger, ed., *Princeton Encyclopedia of Poetry and Poetics*, enlarged ed. (Princeton, N.J.: Princeton University Press, 1974): "The mind rather than the unsupported eye entered the picture."

26. Saussure, *General Linguistics*, 117.

27. Lawson-Peebles ("Williams' *Pictures from Brueghel*," 21) emphasizes the recording function in Williams's reference to "the chronicler." In contrast, I believe Williams has in mind the quality to which Jacob Burckhardt referred when he regretted the loss, in Renaissance histories, of the "life, colour, and brilliancy" of "the earlier chronicles." See Burckhardt, *The Civilization of the Renaissance in Italy*, trans. S. G. C. Middlemore (New York: Harper and Row, 1958), 1: 247. Williams's interest in color constitutes another difference from Pound. See Michael André Bernstein, "Image, Word, and Sign: The Visual Arts as Evidence in Ezra Pound's *Cantos*," *Critical Inquiry* 12 (1986): 358.

28. Derrida, "Différance," *Margins of Philosophy*, trans. Alan Bass (Chicago: University of Chicago Press, 1982), 3.

29. Lawson-Peebles, "Williams' *Pictures from Brueghel*," 21.

30. See fig. 7 for the painting Williams had in mind, *CP2*: 504 for the history of the attribution to Brueghel, no longer accepted by most scholars. Williams's attitude toward craft constitutes one of his ties to the aesthetic of the Precisionist painters. See Weaver, *Williams: American Background*, 58–64; and Peter Schmidt, *William Carlos Williams, the Arts, and Literary Tradition* (Baton Rouge: Louisiana State University Press, 1988), chap. 1. It also constitutes an obstacle to those who would assimilate Williams to a Heideggerian perspective. See Heidegger's dissociation of art and craft in "The Origin of the Work of Art," *Poetry, Language, Thought*, trans. Albert Hofstadter (New York: Harper and Row, 1971), 60–65. Thus, Paul Bové, for

example, concludes it may be necessary to modify Heidegger "by a material consciousness" to do justice to Williams's complexities. See Bové, "The World and Earth of William Carlos Williams: *Paterson* as a 'Long Poem,' " *Genre* 11 (1978): 596.

31. Notes for this passage in the manuscripts reveal a connection between Williams's concern with the quality of "stuff" and the fabric of tapestry: "a tapestry to carry on a life, fabric such / as the mills wove but with less art" (Yale). The Unicorn Tapestries to which Williams refers throughout the published version of *Paterson* 5 supply not only a pattern of imagery but also a material base: "silk and wool shot with silver threads" (*P* 234).

CHAPTER 4

1. Cf. Jacques Lacan, *The Four Fundamental Concepts of Psycho-Analysis*, ed. Jacques-Alain Miller, trans. Alan Sheridan (New York: Norton, 1981), chap. 18, on the role of "the subject who is supposed to know" in psychoanalysis.

2. Williams, "Rome," ed. Steven Ross Loevy, *Iowa Review* 9 (1978): 52. For the clearing of the slums, see also "Midas," *RI* 167; the poem "An Exultation" (1941), *CP2*: 42; and *P* 143. For their connection with Williams's grandmother, see Mariani, *NWN* 452.

3. Arnheim, *The Power of the Center: A Study of Composition in the Visual Arts*, rev. ed. (Berkeley and Los Angeles: University of California Press, 1983), 201. Nikolaus Pevsner, "Bruegel's 'The Adoration of the Kings': 1— The Painter's Message," *The Listener*, 5 Feb. 1945, p. 215, anticipates Arnheim in reading the composition as intentionally oppressive. The rarity of the vertical format in Brueghel's oeuvre was early noted by Georges Hulin de Loo in his catalogue for René van Bastelaer, *Peter Bruegel l'ancien: son oeuvre et son temps* (Brussels: van Oest, 1907), 1: 288.

4. Brueghel's London *Adoration* and *The Massacre of the Innocents* are associated in this context by C. J. Holmes, " 'The Adoration of the Kings' by Pieter Brueghel the Elder," *Burlington Magazine* 38 (1921): 53. Susan E. Blalock ("William Carlos Williams's *Paterson V*: The Damsel, the Virgin, and the Unravished Bride" [Paper delivered at the Twentieth-Century Literature Conference, Literature and the Other Arts, University of Louisville, 28 Feb. 1986]) makes the association in the context of Williams's reading of the London *Adoration*. Pevsner ("Bruegel's 'Adoration' ") fully enumerates relevant events in the Netherlands of Brueghel's day. For a clear pictorial link between the Epiphany and the Massacre, see Jean Fouquet's combination of the two scenes in the *Livre d'Heures d'Étienne Chevalier*, ca. 1450, in Paul Zucker, *Styles in Painting: A Comparative Study* (New York: Viking, 1950), 84.

5. Early drafts specifically, and anachronistically, assign the Soldiers to "the 30 years war" of 1618–48 (Yale).

6. Holmes, " 'Adoration' by Brueghel," 53; Walter Gibson, *Bruegel* (New York: Oxford University Press, 1977), 134. "Hungry eyes" is Holmes's phrase. The figure in question may be "the pop-eyed observer" whom Williams singles out in several early drafts (Yale).

7. A brief reference to the Brueghels in Vienna appears in *VP* 169–70. Although Bosch's name is inscribed on the engraving of *Big Fish Eat Little Fish*, the original pen drawing by Brueghel, signed and dated 1556, has been preserved in the Albertina, Vienna. On the question of attribution, see Louis Lebeer, *Catalogue raisonné des estampes de Bruegel l'ancien* (Brussels: Bibliothèque Royale Albert I, 1969), 56–60.

8. *IAG* 106–7. Another version of this scene appears in *A* 193.

9. *CP2*: 58–59. Literary scholars persist in questioning the identification of *The Kermess*. See, for instance, Stephen C. Behrendt, "Community Relations: The Roles of Artist and Audience in William Carlos Williams's *Pictures from Brueghel*," *American Poetry* 2.2 (1985): 43–45. However, Mazzaro (*LP* 157–58) is correct in citing *The Kermess* as an alternative title for the painting otherwise known as *The Peasant Dance*.

10. The aggressive force of the gaze has undergone extensive analysis in French critical thought, from Sartre to Lacan. Sartre's discussion of seeing as deflowering and devouring in *Being and Nothingness* (trans. Hazel E. Barnes [New York: Washington Square, 1966], 738–39) is especially relevant to the relation between the Soldiers and the Virgin implied by Williams. I deal briefly with Lacan's notion of the gaze in the next chapter.

11. Fig. 10. Christopher MacGowan (*William Carlos Williams's Early Poetry: The Visual Arts Background* [Ann Arbor: UMI Research Press, 1984], 31–33) is especially attentive to the sexual thematics of "March." Schmidt (*Williams, the Arts, and Literary Tradition*, 149–51) finds the poem unresolved, though on different grounds than those I will suggest. On the visual sources of "March," see also Bram Dijkstra, *Cubism, Stieglitz, and the Early Poetry of William Carlos Williams: The Hieroglyphics of a New Speech* (Princeton, N.J.: Princeton University Press, 1969), 60–63; and Dijkstra, "Sight as Censor: William Carlos Williams' 'March' as a Turning Point in the Poet's Career," *Yearbook of Comparative and General Literature* 29 (1980): 10–18. As Dijkstra points out, Angelico's painting is in the convent of San Marco in Florence, not Fiesole, as the poem states. Williams's reference to the three-legged stool on which Mary sits identifies the painting he has in mind as that in the north or upper corridor (ca. 1440), not that in cell 3. However, Mary's submissive posture is typical of Angelico's several treatments of the theme, as noted by Michael Baxandall (*Painting and Experience in Fifteenth-Century Italy: A Primer in the Social History of Pictorial Style* [Oxford: Oxford University Press, 1972], 55).

12. Fig. 11. Dijkstra (*Cubism*, 61) establishes as the main source of this image a relief sculpture from the North Palace of King Ashurbanipal at Nineveh (7th cent. B.C.), now in the British Museum, but points out the complex process to which Williams has submitted this source, including synthesis with the procession of sacred bulls on the Ishtar Gate of Babylon (7th–6th cent. B.C.), now in the Museum für Vor- und Frühgeschichte in Berlin.

13. W. H. Auden, for example, approached the war through Brueghel's *Landscape with the Fall of Icarus* (ca. 1555), John Berryman through *Hunters in the Snow* (1565), and Bertolt Brecht through the *Dulle Griet* (1562). Both *Landscape with the Fall of Icarus* and *Hunters in the Snow* are treated in Williams's "Pictures from Brueghel." The relation of *Landscape with the Fall of*

Icarus to a number of war poems, including Auden's "Musée des Beaux Arts" (1939), is discussed in Robert J. Clements, "Brueghel's *Fall of Icarus*: Eighteen Modern Literary Readings," *Studies in Iconography* 7–8 (1981–82): 253–68. For Berryman's remarks on the relation of his poem "Winter Landscape" (1940) to the war, see Berryman, *The Freedom of the Poet* (New York: Farrar, Straus and Giroux, 1976), 324–26. Brecht thought of Dulle Griet as a model for Grusha in *The Caucasian Chalk Circle* (1948). See notes by Brecht and the editors in Brecht, *Collected Plays*, ed. Ralph Mannheim and John Willett (New York: Random House, Vintage, 1975), 7: 295, 311; see also Brecht's notes entitled "Alienation Effects in the Narrative Pictures of the Elder Brueghel," in *Brecht on Theatre: The Development of an Aesthetic*, trans. John Willett (London: Methuen, 1964), 157–59.

14. *IAG* 174. Such statements offer a useful corrective to the view of Mike Weaver, *William Carlos Williams: The American Background* (Cambridge: Cambridge University Press, 1971), 135–36, on the influence that American violence exercised on Williams.

15. Sandra M. Gilbert and Susan Gubar, *No Man's Land: The Place of the Woman Writer in the Twentieth Century*, vol. 1: *The War of the Words* (New Haven, Conn.: Yale University Press, 1988), 48.

16. For "voyeuristic," see Gilbert and Gubar, *The War of the Words*, 48.

17. Gilbert and Gubar, *The War of the Words*, 49.

18. Cf. the conjunction of "churches and factories" in *Paterson 2* (*P* 56) and Williams's comment on such conjunction in *SL* 258–59.

19. *VP* 13. Dev Evans discovers *Beyond the Pleasure Principle* in a Viennese bookstore in *VP* 181.

20. For the relation of jouissance to the pleasure principle and the death instinct, see, respectively, Jacques Lacan, *Four Fundamental Concepts*, 184; and Lacan, *Ecrits: A Selection*, trans. Alan Sheridan (New York: Norton, 1977), 301, 308. For the shattering of self, see Kristeva, *DL* 142; and Stephen Heath, glossary to Roland Barthes, *Image-Music-Text* (New York: Hill and Wang, 1977), 9. Schmidt (*Williams, the Arts, and Literary Tradition*, 82, 91) applies to Williams a notion of jouissance that is set in opposition to rather than implicated in death and violence.

21. Cf. Williams's acceptance of that in which he has no part in "El Hombre" (1916; *CP1*: 76) and Wallace Stevens's testing of that principle in "Nuances of a Theme by Williams" (1918), in Stevens, *The Palm at the End of the Mind*, ed. Holly Stevens (New York: Random House, Vintage, 1972), 39. Despite their differences, Williams claimed to be "deeply touched" by Stevens's poem (*IWWP* 23).

22. Williams, "Sample Prose Piece: The Three Letters," *Contact* [4 (Summer 1921)]: 10. A further link to the Virgin in *IAG* (26), at the end of the chapter on Columbus, is the quotation from the Latin hymn "Salve Regina," repeated later at the end of the poem Williams addressed to the Virgin, "For Eleanor and Bill Monahan" (1953; *CP2*: 255).

23. Freud occasionally hints at these connections, e.g. "Medusa's Head" (*SE* 18: 273–74), "Female Sexuality" (*SE* 21: 233, 237), but they are developed much more fully by Melanie Klein. See, for example, the triad of essays, "The Psychological Principles of Infant Analysis," "Early Stages of the Oedi-

pus Conflict," and "Infantile Anxiety Situations Reflected in a Work of Art and in the Creative Impulse," in *The Selected Melanie Klein*, ed. Juliet Mitchell (New York: Macmillan, Free Press, 1987), esp. 232n1, 74, 92. Klein's work in this respect serves as the point of departure for recent French psychoanalysts, including Lacan and Kristeva. Cf. Lacan, *Ecrits*, 20–21, and Kristeva, *TL* 32.

24. Freud, "The Uncanny," *SE*17: 231.

25. Freud, "Three Essays," *SE*7: 198; *The Ego and the Id*, *SE*19: 31n1. For the "phallic mother," see especially "Femininity," in the *New Introductory Lectures*, *SE*22: 126, 130.

26. Williams with Stanley Koehler, in *Writers at Work: The* Paris Review *Interviews*, 3d series (New York: Viking, 1967), 12.

27. See esp. *P* 24–25, discussed in chap. 7 below.

28. For Williams's original plan for a four-book poem, see the introductory "Author's Note" to *P*.

29. *P* 202. For the myth, see Hesiod *Theogony* 176–200. MacGowan (*Visual Arts Background*, 8) finds Uranus's castration relevant to another poem by Williams, "From 'The Birth of Venus': Song" (1912; *CP1*: 6).

30. *A* 392, reprinted in "Author's Note" to *P*.

31. Bové, "The World and Earth of William Carlos Williams: *Paterson* as a 'Long Poem,'" *Genre* 11 (1978): 592.

32. Deriving the phrase from the title of Céline's novel *D'un chateau l'autre*, Kristeva employs it as the title of her essay on identity in *DL* and scatters it throughout her discussion of Céline in *PH*, e.g. 161, 164, 165.

33. Mariani traces the complicated history of *Paterson* 5 in *NWN*. The poem that Williams started in early 1952, two years after completing *Paterson* 4, turned into "Asphodel" (645). What we now have as *Paterson* 5 was not begun until 1956 (693). In Mariani's judgment, however, "*Paterson* 5—the book of the Woman—had quietly insisted on being written as early as January 1950, even as Williams began thinking of *Paterson* 4 and the original close of his poem" (697).

CHAPTER 5

1. Wolfgang Stechow, *Pieter Bruegel the Elder* (New York: Abrams, [1970]), 92. On the humanizing tendency in Franciscan representation, see Kristeva, *TL* 246–48. For sexuality in Brueghel's London *Adoration* specifically, see Leo Steinberg, *The Sexuality of Christ in Renaissance Art and in Modern Oblivion* (New York: Pantheon, 1983), 67, 166; more generally, Meyer Schapiro, " 'Muscipula Diaboli,' The Symbolism of the Merode Altarpiece," in Schapiro, *Late Antique, Early Christian and Medieval Art* (New York: Braziller, 1979), 1–19.

2. Lowell, review of *Paterson* 2, in Jerome Mazzaro, ed., *Profile of William Carlos Williams* (Columbus, Ohio: Merrill, 1971), 75.

3. Cf. John Malcolm Brinnin, *William Carlos Williams* (Minneapolis: University of Minnesota Press, 1963), 16.

4. Williams, "Prose About Love," *Little Review* 6.2 (1918): 9.

5. Susan R. Suleiman and Inge Crosman, "Preface," in Suleiman and Crosman, eds., *The Reader in the Text: Essays on Audience and Interpretation* (Princeton, N.J.: Princeton University Press, 1980), vii. I began to explore an alternative to this view in Terence Diggory, "The Reader in Williams and Brueghel: *Paterson* 5 and *The Adoration of the Kings*," *Criticism* 30 (1988): 349–73.

6. Bram Dijkstra, *Cubism, Stieglitz, and the Early Poetry of William Carlos Williams: The Hieroglyphics of a New Speech* (Princeton, N.J.: Princeton University Press, 1969), 68–69; Mazzaro, *LP*, chap. 2; Peter Schmidt, *William Carlos Williams, the Arts, and Literary Tradition* (Baton Rouge: Louisiana State University Press, 1988), 48.

7. William Carlos Williams to Edgar Williams, 6 April 1909, quoted in William Marling, *William Carlos Williams and the Painters, 1909–1923* (Athens: Ohio University Press, 1982), 18–19.

8. Williams's romantic version of the Curies' story seems to have been influenced by the MGM film *Madame Curie*, which Williams saw in 1944. See Mariani, *NWN* 492.

9. *P* 177. As Mike Weaver notes (*William Carlos Williams: The American Background* [Cambridge: Cambridge University Press, 1971], 214), Williams's reference is to H. Levy, *A Philosophy for Modern Man* (New York: Knopf, 1938). Under the heading "antagonistic cooperation," however, Weaver (137–44) does not discuss Levy but rather Williams's adaptation of the "dialectical method" of surrealism. Riddel (*IB* 33–34) gives an extended note on Levy.

10. See *VT* 62–63 for Sayre's association of opposition and the sexual relation.

11. "A Sort of a Song" (1943), *CP2*: 55.

12. Mariani, "The Eighth Day of Creation: Rethinking *Paterson*," in Mariani, *A Usable Past: Essays on Modern and Contemporary Poetry* (Amherst: University of Massachusetts Press, 1984), 69.

13. The attenuation of the man's role in this process begins in Mariani, "Eighth Day of Creation" (72), where the male is identified as the artist but subordinated as "the lesser figure" in relation to the woman as work of art.

14. Williams, "Letter to an Australian Editor," *Briarcliff Quarterly* 3.11 (1946): 207–8. Richard Sieburth ("In Pound We Trust: The Economy of Poetry/The Poetry of Economics," *Critical Inquiry* 14 [1987]: 164) alludes to the Immaculate Conception. Mazzaro (*LP* 115, 117, 122) explicitly identifies Williams's aesthetic as androgynous, an identification to which Bram Dijkstra (introduction to *RI* 46 n26) objects.

15. On the other hand, this recognition provides Joseph Riddel's point of departure in *IB* 15–16.

16. *LM* 161. Williams's divergence from Brueghel in this respect is also noted by Riddel (*IB* 275, 292, and *Glyph* 225–26) and Ulrich Bachteler (*Die Darstellung von Werken der Malerei in der amerikanischen Lyrik des 20. Jahrhunderts* [Frankfurt/Main: R. G. Fischer, 1979], 197).

17. Williams was finally able to fix his focus on Joseph by referring only to him as an "old man." From the earliest drafts Joseph is located in the center

of the composition, but initially his age fails to distinguish him from the Wise Men. The lines in the published version about "the unkempt straggling / hair of the old man in the / middle" began as a broader reference to "the unkempt straggling hair / of the old men," grouping Joseph with the Wise Men (Yale).

18. For more on the "Self-Portrait" as a depiction of Williams, see Joel Conarroe, "The Measured Dance: Williams' 'Pictures from Brueghel,' " *Journal of Modern Literature* 1 (1971): 571; and Stephen C. Behrendt, "Community Relations: The Roles of Artist and Audience in William Carlos Williams's *Pictures from Brueghel,*" *American Poetry* 2.2 (1985): 33.

19. For that threat, see Mariani, *NWN* 635, 663. In the manuscript from which both "Asphodel" and *Paterson* 5 evolved, "old men / because they are sterile" appear first in a list of "things . . . opposed / to the present monomania of the world" (Yale). The other two things are "gardens" and "the sea." In the published version of "Asphodel," this passage survives in the form of a celebration of Homer as "a sexless old man" (*CP2*: 322).

20. *LM* 15–17. Mazzaro cites "Archetypes of the Collective Unconscious" and "The Phenomenology of the Spirit in Fairytales," in Jung, *Psyche and Symbol,* ed. Violet S. de Laszlo (Garden City, N.Y.: Doubleday, Anchor, 1952). Cf. Jung, "Psychology and Poetry," trans. Eugene Jolas, *transition* 19–20 (June 1930): 44, for a discussion of the "wise man" archetype in an essay Williams is known to have read, as noted below.

21. *SL* xvii. "Caviar and Bread Again" appears in *SE* 102–4, and refers to Jung, "Psychology and Poetry." See Mariani, *NWN* 307. A different translation appears as the chapter "Psychology and Literature" in Jung, *Modern Man in Search of a Soul,* trans. W. S. Dell and Cary F. Baynes (New York: Harcourt, Brace and World, n.d.), 152–72.

22. Jung, "Psychology and Poetry," 41.

23. In 1947, long after his initial enthusiasm for Jung had faded, Williams was still seeking a theory to oppose to Freud's, this time in Wilhelm Reich, theorist of the orgasm. See Mariani, *NWN* 534, 537. For some statements by Williams on writing as release or relief, in addition to the statement in connection with Freud quoted below, see *CP1*: 208, 235; *I* 289; *P* 113; *RI* 221.

24. Lacan, *The Four Fundamental Concepts of Psycho-Analysis,* ed. Jacques-Alain Miller, trans. Alan Sheridan (New York: Norton, 1981), 165. Cf. Leo Bersani, *The Freudian Body: Psychoanalysis and Art* (New York: Columbia University Press, 1986), 45, 120n10.

25. Two of these images were combined in early versions of "For Eleanor and Bill Monahan" (1953), where the moon was identified as "Venus'." See *CP2*: 487.

26. *CP1*: 35, 29. This text is that of the first published version (1914).

27. James Guimond, *The Art of William Carlos Williams: A Discovery and Possession of America* (Urbana: University of Illinois Press, 1968), 15; Kerry Driscoll, *William Carlos Williams and the Maternal Muse* (Ann Arbor: UMI Research Press, 1987), 6–7.

28. See Kristeva on "oralization" and poetic language, *RPL* 153–54. Although my emphasis in this chapter is on the fluidity of personal identity, I would apply the same principle to the fluidity of grammatical identity examined in chap. 3.

29. Gilbert, "Purloined Letters: William Carlos Williams and 'Cress,'"
William Carlos Williams Review 11.2 (1985): 13; this argument is incorporated in Sandra M. Gilbert and Susan Gubar, *No Man's Land: The Place of the Woman Writer in the Twentieth Century*, vol. 1: *The War of the Words* (New Haven, Conn.: Yale University Press, 1988), 153.

30. For Gilbert and Bloom, see Sandra M. Gilbert and Susan Gubar, *The Madwoman in the Attic: The Woman Writer and the Nineteenth-Century Literary Imagination* (New Haven, Conn.: Yale University Press, 1979), 46–53; for Freud, "Dostoevsky and Parricide," *SE*21: 183–86.

31. Gilbert, "Purloined Letters," 7. For Freud on the oral stage and the mother's breast as object, see "Three Essays on Sexuality," *SE*7: 198, 222.

32. Freud, "Group Psychology and the Analysis of the Ego," *SE*18: 106.

33. "Nonobject" is Kristeva's term for what she otherwise calls the "abject." See *PH* 46; *TL* 26, 41. For relevant texts in Freud, see "Three Essays on Sexuality," *SE*7: 198; *The Ego and the Id*, *SE*19: 30–31. For the difficulty posed by Freud's speculation, see J. Laplanche and J.-B. Pontalis, *The Language of Psychoanalysis*, trans. Donald Nicholson-Smith (New York: Norton, 1973), s.v. "Primary Identification."

34. Gilbert, "Purloined Letters," 12.

35. Williams, "An Approach to the Poem," *English Institute Essays 1947* (New York: Columbia University Press, 1948), 56. Cf. Archibald MacLeish, "Ars Poetica" (1926): "A poem should not mean / But be" (MacLeish, *New and Collected Poems, 1917–1976* [Boston: Houghton Mifflin, 1976], 107).

36. These concerns circulate vertiginously in the left-hand column of "Stabat Mater," e.g. *TL* 240, but are elsewhere treated more analytically, even within that column; see, for instance, the discussion of "women's discourse" and intonation, *TL* 257, 259. Because she views it as a special relation to the symbolic function of language, rather than as a realm absolutely separate from that function, Kristeva insists on distinguishing her notion of "women's discourse" from the notion of *écriture féminine* propounded by Hélène Cixous. See Kristeva with Françoise van Rossum-Guyon, "À partir de *Polylogue*," *Revue des sciences humaines* 168 (1977): 496; Kristeva, "Women's Time," *KR* 207. For the analogy of color in painting and rhythm in poetry, see "Giotto's Joy," *DL* 221–22, 235n12.

37. Lacan, *Four Fundamental Concepts*, 74; "The Mirror Stage," *Ecrits: A Selection*, trans. Alan Sheridan (New York: Norton, 1977), 1–7. In *Four Fundamental Concepts*, 89, Lacan declares that any picture is "a trap for the gaze." Metaphors of capture and a tendency to favor speech over image persist as part of Kristeva's inheritance from Lacan, even as she attempts to distinguish her own position. See *TL* 37, 43.

38. John C. Thirlwall ("William Carlos Williams' 'Paterson,'" *New Directions* 17 [1961]: 254) quotes Williams on "redeeming language." For Lacan on language and the "name of the father," see esp. "The Function and Field of Speech and Language in Psychoanalysis," *Ecrits*, 65–67.

39. For the celebration of women as an aim of *Paterson* 5, see Williams to Charles Tomlinson, 12 July 1958, quoted by Mariani, *NWN* 842n23.

40. For Lacan, it is "desire," as distinct from Kristeva's "love," that "finds its meaning in the desire of the other" (*Ecrits*, 58). For the distinction, see *TL*

30, 38. Kristeva here explicitly disagrees with Lacan over the role of primary identification. Cf. Lacan, *Four Fundamental Concepts*, 256.

41. Lacan, *Four Fundamental Concepts*, 88–90, 92. I have benefited from Alan Durant's discussion of Lacan on Holbein, in *Ezra Pound, Identity in Crisis* (Totowa, N.J.: Barnes and Noble, 1981), 82–84.

CHAPTER 6

1. My source for the biographical detail in this and the next paragraph is chap. 13 of Mariani, *NWN*.

2. Diane Ward Ashton ("The Virgin-Whore Motif in William Carlos Williams' *Paterson*," *Modern Poetry Studies* 4.2 [1973]: 196) identifies the figure in "The Wanderer" as "the earliest manifestation of the virgin-whore image." Ashton's study is more focused and more reliable than Audrey T. Rodgers, *Virgin and Whore: The Image of Women in the Poetry of William Carlos Williams* (Jefferson, N.C.: McFarland, 1987).

3. *DL* 247. Kristeva's analysis of the remoteness of the gaze in Bellini's Madonnas can be profitably compared with Griselda Pollock's analysis of a similar phenomenon in a series of women painted by Dante Gabriel Rossetti. See Pollock, *Vision and Difference: Femininity, Feminism and Histories of Art* (London: Routledge, 1988), 125–28, 133–34, 146.

4. See Miller, *LM* 349. Although Miller intends to correct this view, his interpretation of Williams preserves the impression of transparency to a remarkable degree.

5. Sandra M. Gilbert, "Purloined Letters: William Carlos Williams and 'Cress' "; Stephen Tapscott, "Williams, Sappho, and the Woman-as-Other": both in the special number on Williams and women of the *William Carlos Williams Review* 11.2 (1985): 8, 40.

6. Kerry Driscoll, *William Carlos Williams and the Maternal Muse* (Ann Arbor: UMI Research Press, 1987), 7; my emphasis.

7. *LM* 387, 360. For Derrida, of course, to delay "ever so slightly" would be more than enough, but Miller's deconstruction of Williams tends to minimize such excess. For Miller's earlier commitment to immediacy, see *PR* 10.

8. See Riddel, *IB*, and Sayre, *VT*. Riddel elaborates on his preference for *Paterson* 5 over "Asphodel" in *IB* 200. See Tapscott, "Williams, Sappho," 39–40, for his attempt to overcome the obstacle of *Paterson* 5 and for the assignment of "writing" to the visual pole of his progression.

9. Tapscott, "Williams, Sappho," 39. On p. 35, Tapscott misidentifies Charles Abbott as the source of the statement about Sappho's "clear gentle tinkling voice" that Williams places at the head of his translation of Sappho (*P* 217). The statement appears over the initials "A. P.," for Arnold Post, a professor of classics whom Williams consulted during his work on the translation. See Mike Weaver, *William Carlos Williams: The American Background* (Cambridge: Cambridge University Press, 1971), 217–18; and Mariani, *NWN* 709–10.

10. The first charge is made by Bram Dijkstra, introduction to *RI* 45n26, who uses the term "sexist" to characterize Williams's essay (*RI* 36). The sec-

ond charge is made by Joan Nay, who takes "Woman as Operator" as her starting point in "William Carlos Williams and the Singular Woman" (*William Carlos Williams Review* 11.2 [1985]: 45–54). Seeing coercion where Williams sees permission, Nay (46) misquotes Williams as saying the artist "must abstract" from woman, whereas Williams wrote that he "can abstract" (*RI* 181).

11. In this respect, I believe Williams's essay on Bearden is comparable to Griselda Pollock's on Rossetti, in Pollock, *Vision and Difference*, chap. 6, which examines "the negotiation of masculine sexuality in an order in which woman is the sign, not of woman, but of that Other in whose mirror masculinity must define itself" (153).

12. *RI* 181. A similar argument appears in Williams's earlier essay, "The Great Sex Spiral," part 2, *Egoist* [4.7] (1917): 110–11, which also elicits Dijkstra's charge of sexism (*RI* 45–46n26). Though it goes further in a speculative attempt to characterize both male and female experience, "The Great Sex Spiral" agrees with "Woman as Operator" in the basic premise that neither sex can finally know the experience of the other.

13. "The Portrait: Emanuel Romano" (1951), *RI* 197. In "French Painting," too, Williams declared, "All painting is representation and cannot be anything else" (*RI* 69). Although Williams's usage contradicts the common understanding that holds "abstract" to be synonymous with "nonrepresentational," Harold Osborne's careful attempt to disentangle the many meanings of "abstraction" in modern art offers support for Williams's logic. Osborne (*Abstraction and Artifice in Twentieth-Century Art* [Oxford: Oxford University Press, 1979], 11) quotes a statement by Juan Gris that may well have been a source for Williams's position: "the only purpose of any picture is to achieve representation." I discuss Gris as a source for Williams in the next chapter.

14. Williams, "A Poet Who Cannot Pause," rev. René Char, *Hypnos Waking*, *New Republic*, 17 Sept. 1956, 18; reprinted in *Something to Say: William Carlos Williams on Younger Poets*, ed. James E. B. Breslin (New York: New Directions, 1985), 219-20. Bosch remains an example in "Tribute to the Painters," discussed below. In stressing the continuity Williams saw between modern and traditional painting, I am agreeing with Henry Sayre's rebuttal (*VT* 132–33) of those critics who see the late Williams as turning his back on his earlier commitment to modern art, e.g., Marjorie Perloff, *The Poetics of Indeterminacy: Rimbaud to Cage* (Princeton, N.J.: Princeton University Press, 1981), 151, 153.

15. *P* 222. For relevant discussion of "Tribute to the Painters," see Alexander Hutchison, "The Resourceful Mind: William Carlos Williams and 'Tribute to the Painters,'" *University of Windsor Review* 8 (1972): 81–89; Henry Sayre, "The Tyranny of the Image: The Aesthetic Background," *William Carlos Williams Review* 9.1–2 (1983): 125–34; and Emily Mitchell Wallace, "The Satyrs' Abstract and Brief Chronicle of Our Time," *William Carlos Williams Review* 9.1–2 (1983): 136–54.

16. *P* 222, 119. Peter Schmidt (" 'These': Williams' Deepest Descent," *William Carlos Williams Review* 9.1–2 [1983]: 74–90) discusses the theme of melancholy in Williams with reference to Dürer. The theme suggests an

approach to Williams complementary to the approach through the theme of love that I have undertaken here. The complementary approach might take its bearings from the early depressive episode Williams described as his "nameless religious experience" (*SL* 147), and the later one suffered while *Paterson* 5 was in gestation. Julia Kristeva (*Black Sun: Depression and Melancholia*, trans. Leon S. Roudiez [New York: Columbia University Press, 1989]) suggests a theoretical framework, similar to the one *TL* offers the present study.

17. For an early statement on the "unrelatedness" of titles as an aesthetic principle, see Williams to Harriet Monroe, 5 March 1913, *SL* 24. I am grateful to Carl Rapp for bringing this letter to my attention.

18. For Gauguin and abstraction, see the excerpt from his letter to Emile Schuffenecker, 14 August 1888, in Herschel B. Chipp, ed., *Theories of Modern Art: A Source Book by Artists and Critics* (Berkeley and Los Angeles: University of California Press, 1971), 60. See also Osborne, *Abstraction and Artifice*, 47–48.

19. The following account of *The Spirit of the Dead Watching* is based on Jean de Rotonchamp, *Paul Gauguin 1848–1903*, new ed. (Paris: Crès, 1925), 218–20, trans. in Chipp, ed., *Theories of Modern Art*, 67–69. Rotonchamp (81) is also the authority for the "provisional" title of *The Loss of Virginity*, but in the original French the title, *La Perte du pucelage*, uses a term subtly different from *virginité* and one without an English equivalent. For a deconstructive play upon the difference between *virginité* and *pucelage*, see Jacques Derrida, *Of Grammatology*, trans. Gayatri Chakravorty Spivak (Baltimore: Johns Hopkins University Press, 1976), 150.

20. Denys Sutton, "*La Perte du Pucelage* by Paul Gauguin," *Burlington Magazine* 91 (1949): 105; Rotonchamp, *Gauguin*, 82; Wayne Anderson, *Gauguin's Paradise Lost* (New York: Viking, 1971), 103. The symbolic reading of the fox is Gauguin's, though in reference to another work, *Be in Love, You Will Be Happy* (1889).

21. Gauguin to Charles Morice, July 1901, in Chipp, ed., *Theories of Modern Art*, 66; discussed in Anderson, *Gauguin's Paradise Lost*, 104.

22. See Wayne Anderson, "Gauguin's Motifs at Le Pouldu—Preliminary Report," *Burlington Magazine* 112 (1970): 615–20.

23. Chipp, ed., *Theories of Modern Art*, 69.

24. Jacques Derrida, "The Double Session," *Dissemination*, trans. Barbara Johnson (Chicago: University of Chicago Press, 1981), 177–80.

25. Derrida, *Spurs: Nietzsche's Styles*, trans. Barbara Harlow (Chicago: University of Chicago Press, 1979), 52–53. The first quotation is my own translation of the French text.

26. In which gallery and at what date Williams saw Matisse's painting are questions open to debate. Cf. Mariani, *NWN* 175, and William Marling, *William Carlos Williams and the Painters, 1909–1923* (Athens: Ohio University Press, 1982), 89.

27. *P* 222. For Gauguin and Matisse, see Osborne, *Abstraction and Artifice*, 35, 48; and Pierre Schneider, *Matisse*, trans. Michael Taylor and Bridget Strevens Romer (New York: Rizzoli, 1984), 255–57. For the *Blue Nude* and Islamic art, see Schneider, *Matisse*, 158.

28. Schneider, *Matisse*, 348–49. In a revised version of his study of "A

Matisse" (*Painterly Abstraction in Modernist American Poetry: The Contemporaneity of Modernism* [Cambridge: Cambridge University Press, 1989], 20–24), Altieri surprisingly, and unaccountably, declares the *Blue Nude* to be a portrait of "Bishkra," whom he identifies as Matisse's Algerian mistress, though the "Biskra" in the painting's subtitle, as Schneider confirms (158), refers to the Algerian oasis that Matisse visited in 1906.

29. *Dada* 116. Altieri does not treat Picasso's *Demoiselles* in *Painterly Abstraction*. Jack Flam (*Matisse: The Man and His Art 1869–1918* [Ithaca, N.Y.: Cornell University Press, 1986], 196, 217) sees the *Demoiselles* as a response to the *Blue Nude*.

30. Riddel attempts to relate Williams to Hegel's theme of desire in *IB* 25n18. Though Altieri appears to favor Kant in *Painterly Abstraction*, Hegel features in the conclusion of both *AQ* and *Dada*, as well as in the following aside: "One might almost say Picasso has painted Hegel's master-slave relationship" (*Dada* 115). The section on master and slave, along with the preceding section on "The Truth of Self-Certainty," constitutes the principal discussion of desire in Hegel, *Phenomenology of Spirit*, trans. A. V. Miller (Oxford: Oxford University Press, 1977), 104–19.

31. *TL* 29–31, 36–38. Kristeva can be seen beginning to move outside the circle of desire in *RPL* 145–46. For Lacan on Hegel, see esp. "The Subversion of the Subject and the Dialectic of Desire in the Freudian Unconscious," *Ecrits: A Selection*, trans. Alan Sheridan (New York: Norton, 1977), 301, 307–9. Judith P. Butler (*Subjects of Desire: Hegelian Reflections in Twentieth-Century France* [New York: Columbia University Press, 1987]) treats both Lacan and Kristeva, noting in the latter "a significant departure from the Hegelian program" (233).

32. Lacan, "Aggressivity in Psychoanalysis," *Ecrits*, 18; *Dada* 111.

33. "One searches the 'Blue Nude' in vain for such foliage—Williams invented it," according to Marling (*Williams and the Painters*, 90). However, discussing the picture's relation to Biskra, Schneider (*Matisse*, 158) states, "The only note of 'local color' in the picture is the palm trees in the background."

34. Aside from the essay on Bellini discussed here, other especially relevant essays by Kristeva are "Giotto's Joy" and "Place Names," both in *DL*. Mary Jacobus, *Reading Woman: Essays in Feminist Criticism*, pt. 3, chap. 1, offers a full examination of this theme in Kristeva's work in the context of current feminist theory.

35. See fig. 21. On the *hortus conclusus*, see Margaret R. Freeman, *The Unicorn Tapestries* (New York: Metropolitan Museum of Art, 1976), 136. For the traditions discussed below, see also John Williamson, *The Oak King, the Holly King, and the Unicorn: The Myths and Symbolism of the Unicorn Tapestries* (New York: Harper and Row, 1986).

36. Drafts for *Paterson* 5 describe the unicorn as "love's captive" and assume "its masculinity / plain to see" (Yale). Riddel cites Ernest Jones in support of the phallic symbolism of the unicorn (IB 279) and discusses the unicorn as "a supernatural erection" (*Glyph* 214). Mariani (*NWN* 697) also attributes phallic symbolism to the unicorn.

37. In their search for a place outside desire, deconstructionists have shown an increasing tendency to appeal to the notion of necessity or law, an alternative very different from the notion of love that I am exploring in Williams and Kristeva. See Jacques Derrida, *The Ear of the Other: Otobiography, Transference, Translation*, ed. Christie V. McDonald, trans. Peggy Kamuf (New York: Schocken, 1985), 115–16. See also the role of law in Miller (*ER*) discussed in the next chapter.

CHAPTER 7

1. Hans-Georg Gadamer, "Text and Interpretation," in Diane P. Michelfelder and Richard E. Palmer, eds., *Dialogue and Deconstruction: The Gadamer-Derrida Encounter* (Albany: State University of New York Press, 1989), 33, 24. This volume assembles the texts of an exchange between Gadamer and Jacques Derrida at the Goethe Institute in Paris in April 1981. As the editors note (52), the title of Derrida's response to Gadamer as originally published in both French and German included the phrase "good-will-to-power" that I employ below.

2. Edmond Jabès with Richard Stamelman, "On Dialogue and the Other," *Studies in Twentieth-Century Literature* 12 (1987): 37.

3. Derrida frames this last question with his translation of Husserl's *bedeuten*, "to mean," as *vouloir dire*, "to want to say." See Derrida, *Speech and Phenomena and Other Essays on Husserl's Theory of Signs*, trans. David B. Allison (Evanston, Ill.: Northwestern University Press, 1973), 18.

4. Deconstruction can be viewed as a continuation of the New Criticism in this respect. See Cleanth Brooks, "What Does Poetry Communicate?" *The Well Wrought Urn: Studies in the Structure of Poetry* (New York: Harcourt, Brace and World, 1947), 67–79.

5. Kristeva's acceptance of the "death drive" leads her to postulate an original violence that is sublimated in the dynamics of love. See *RPL* 149–50; *TL* 14–15, 233.

6. Gadamer, "Reply to Jacques Derrida," in Michelfelder and Palmer, eds., *Dialogue and Deconstruction*, 55–56.

7. Derrida, *The Ear of the Other: Otobiography, Transference, Translation*, ed. Christie V. McDonald, trans. Peggy Kamuf (New York: Schocken, 1985), 107. Derrida's remarks here are his most concise summary of the critique mounted in his more famous essay, "Le facteur de la vérité," *The Post Card: From Socrates to Freud and Beyond*, trans. Alan Bass (Chicago: University of Chicago Press, 1987), 411–96.

8. *TL* 93. Kristeva locates her position "midway" between classical interpretation and deconstruction in "Psychoanalysis and the Polis" (*KR* 306). See also the editor's introduction to that essay (301). For Gadamer's constrasting view of dialogue, see esp. Gadamer, *Truth and Method* (New York: Seabury, 1975), 325–33.

9. Whitaker, "To Dance a Measure" (Paper delivered at the conference on "William Carlos Williams and the 'American Style,' " William Patterson Col-

lege, Wayne, N.J., 15 April 1988). I am grateful to Professor Whitaker for furnishing a typescript of this paper. Whitaker alludes to Gadamer in the context of Williams in "*Spring and All*: Teaching Us the Figures of the Dance," *William Carlos Williams Review* 10.2 (1984): 3, 6.

10. For Kristeva on an inaccessible "elsewhere," see *DL* 247, 285; *RPL* 100; *KR* 317; on imagination, *TL* 24, 45, 90.

11. Gadamer, *Truth and Method*, 349.

12. Gadamer, *Truth and Method*, 352.

13. Williams, "An Approach to the Poem," *English Institute Essays 1947* (New York: Columbia University Press, 1948), 50. Cf. *A* 264–65.

14. *A Novelette* was written in 1929 but not published until 1932. Rather than referring to this work as *January: A Novelette*, as it is sometimes known, I have followed the practice of Webster Schott, editor of *I*, where the work is reprinted in full (272–306). The section entitled "Conversation as Design" forms part of "The Simplicity of Disorder" in *SE* 98–101. Whitaker refers to "conversation as design" in *William Carlos Williams* (New York: Twayne, 1968), 95–96; "Conversation as Design," rev. *RI*, *William Carlos Williams Newsletter* 5.2 (1979): 26–27; "Conversation as Design," *Profession 84* (Modern Language Association of America): 3; "*Spring and All*: Teaching Us the Figures of the Dance," 3; and "To Dance a Measure."

15. Whitaker's objection (*William Carlos Williams Newsletter* 5.2 [1979]: 27n6) is aimed specifically at Rob Fure, "The Design of Experience: William Carlos Williams and Juan Gris" (*William Carlos Williams Newsletter* 4.2 [1978]: 10–19), but would apply also, I believe, to Henry Sayre in *VT*, as I will explain below.

16. Quoted by Fure, "The Design of Experience," 15. The original French version of the essay would have been available to Williams in two numbers of the *transatlantic review*, June and July 1924. Fure (19n9) acknowledges the chronological gap between this date and that of Williams's *Autobiography*. "Formal Necessities" is the title of the first chapter in *VT*, in which Sayre discusses Williams's relation to Gris. Sayre's book as a whole argues that Williams finally abandoned an aesthetic of "synthesis" (9), associated with Gris, in favor of an aesthetic of "heterogeneity" (94, 115n1). In my view, however, Williams's aesthetic was more "heterogeneous" to begin with, and Sayre's reading of his relation to Gris is evidence of Sayre's own inclination toward the formalist view of "design" that he claims Williams set out from. Christopher MacGowan's discussion of Gris in connection with Williams's practice of "dispassionately realizing discrete particulars" is closer to my understanding of Williams's claim that Brueghel served the imagination "dispassionately." See MacGowan, *William Carlos Williams's Early Poetry: The Visual Arts Background* (Ann Arbor: UMI Research Press, 1984), 108.

17. *CP1*: 195, 197. Critics debate whether "The Rose" refers to a specific collage by Gris. See Henry M. Sayre, "Distancing 'The Rose' from *Roses*," *William Carlos Williams Newsletter* 4.1 (1979): 18–19.

18. Michel Oren ("Williams and Gris: A Borrowed Aesthetic," *Contemporary Literature* 26 [1985]: 203) suggests that this passage refers to Gris's *Still*

Life, reproduced in *Broom* 1.1 (1921), but the relation between still life and landscape elements in Williams's description leads me to believe that, as in *Spring and All,* he was thinking of *The Open Window,* reproduced in *Broom* 1.3 (1922).

19. Whitaker, *William Carlos Williams Newsletter* 5.2 (1979): 27.

20. On Stein's motto, see Richard Bridgman, *Gertrude Stein in Pieces* (New York: Oxford University Press, 1970), 138–39, 300. The motto first appears, though not in circular form, in Stein, "Sacred Emily," *Geography & Plays* (Boston: Four Seas, 1922), 187. Stein used the circular format on her letterhead, which Williams may have seen in connection with his visit to her in Paris in 1927 (on which see *A* 253–54; Mariani, *NWN* 261). The circular printing on the cover of *The Autobiography of Alice B. Toklas* (New York: Harcourt, Brace, 1933) postdates Williams's essay on "French Painting" (1928). Williams incorporated the motto in the "River of Heaven" manuscript from which both "Asphodel" and *Paterson* 5 emerged (Yale; Sayre, *VT* 119). A reference to Stein remains in the "Tribute to the Painters" section of *Paterson* 5 (*P* 222; *CP2*: 296).

21. See Miller, *PR* 308–9, *LM* 379, for a similar point based on texts from *Spring and All.*

22. Mike Weaver (*William Carlos Williams: The American Background* [Cambridge: Cambridge University Press, 1971], 41–42) quotes a passage from Gris's "On the Possibilities of Painting" to which he assumes Williams's remarks refer.

23. Whitaker, *William Carlos Williams Newsletter* 5.2 (1979): 27. For an explicit link between ethics and humanism, posed as a challenge to the anti-humanism of deconstruction, see Tobin Siebers, *The Ethics of Criticism* (Ithaca, N.Y.: Cornell University Press, 1988), 217–19, 225, 239–40.

24. Whitaker, "To Dance a Measure"; "*Spring and All*: Teaching Us the Figures of the Dance," 1. For a similar reading, see Thomas H. Jackson, "Positivism and Modern Poetics: Yeats, Mallarmé, and William Carlos Williams," *ELH* 46 (1979): 538.

25. James, *The Art of the Novel: Critical Prefaces* (Boston: Northeastern University Press, 1984), 336, quoted in Miller, *ER* 111.

26. James, *The Art of the Novel,* 336, quoted in Miller, *ER* 116.

27. See Rudolf Arnheim, *Art and Visual Perception: A Psychology of the Creative Eye* (Berkeley and Los Angeles: University of California Press, 1969), 218.

28. For "translation . . . both necessary and impossible," see Derrida, *The Ear of the Other,* 103.

29. Hegel, *Logic,* trans. William Wallace (Oxford: Oxford University Press, 1975), 31. Irene E. Harvey (*Derrida and the Economy of* Différance [Bloomington: Indiana University Press, 1986], 107, 251n37) cites this passage with reference to deconstruction.

30. In the introductory section of *TL,* Kristeva makes particular reference to Freud's "The Dynamics of Transference" and "Observations on Transference-Love" (*SE* 12: 99–108; 159–71).

31. Hartman, *Saving the Text: Literature/Derrida/Philosophy* (Baltimore: Johns Hopkins University Press, 1982), 17. Derrida's essay on Adami is "+R (Into the Bargain)," *The Truth in Painting*, trans. Geoff Bennington and Ian MacLeod (Chicago: University of Chicago Press, 1987), 149–82. A number of commentators have set Derrida's attitude toward images within a tradition of iconoclasm, whether specifically Jewish or more broadly Western. For the former position, see Hartman, *Saving the Text*, 17; Susan Handelman, *The Slayers of Moses: The Emergence of Rabbinic Interpretation in Modern Literary Theory* (Albany: State University of New York Press, 1982), 118; Handelman, "Jacques Derrida and the Heretic Hermeneutic," in Mark Krupnick, ed., *Displacement: Derrida and After* (Bloomington: Indiana University Press, 1983), 107. For the latter position, see Ernest Gilman, *Iconoclasm and Poetry in the English Reformation: Down Went Dagon* (Chicago: University of Chicago Press, 1986), 191; W.J.T. Mitchell, *Iconology: Image, Text, Ideology* (Chicago: University of Chicago Press, 1986), 30. Carl Rapp (*William Carlos Williams and Romantic Idealism* [Hanover, N.H.: University Press of New England, 1984], 33–38) emphasizes the importance of the Western iconoclastic tradition to Williams, where I would emphasize Williams's difference from that tradition.

32. Derrida, *Writing and Difference*, trans. Alan Bass (Chicago: University of Chicago Press, 1978), 209–210. Cf. Freud on "perceptual residues" ("The Unconscious," *SE*14: 201–4), used by Kristeva against Derrida (*RPL* 144).

33. Derrida, "Différance," *Margins of Philosophy*, trans. Alan Bass (Chicago: University of Chicago Press, 1982), 5. "Sensible Language" is a section heading in Krupnick, ed., *Displacement*, 21ff. Cf. the critique of "materiality" outlined in Hillis Miller, "The Triumph of Theory, the Resistance to Reading, and the Question of the Material Base," 1986 Presidential Address, Modern Language Association of America, *PMLA* 102 (1987): 281–91, which finds its starting point in Williams (*IAG*).

34. Mitchell (*Iconology*, 109, 112) connects the theme of adultery with theories that oppose the mixture of the arts. Peter Schmidt (*William Carlos Williams, the Arts, and Literary Tradition* [Baton Rouge: Louisiana State University Press, 1988], 248–49) sets Williams's interest in the other arts against "his tortured constancy to literary tradition," drawing a parallel to the "tortured constancy" to his wife that Williams professes in "To Be Recited to Flossie on Her Birthday" (1961; *CP2*: 410).

35. The difference between Kristeva and Derrida on the issue of materiality may be accounted for in part by Kristeva's nomination of Jakobson as the central figure in modern linguistics, whereas Derrida would nominate Saussure. Derrida contrasts these linguists in *Of Grammatology*, trans. Gayatri Chakravorty Spivak (Baltimore: Johns Hopkins University Press, 1976), 53–55. On the other hand, the importance to Kristeva of the Russian futurist poets, with whom Jakobson was closely allied, helps to mark the difference between Kristeva and Williams. Much of "The Ethics of Linguistics" is devoted to the poetry of Mayakovsky and Khlebnikov. In *Spring and All* (*CP1*: 235), Williams rejects the Russian futurists' experiments with "unoriented

sounds in place of conventional words," as Miller (*LM* 378) is pleased to note. However, upon meeting Mayakovsky in person in 1925, Williams was much impressed. See *CP2*: 146; *A* 163; Mariani, *NWN* 247–48.

36. *TL* 91. For more on the cathexis of signs, see esp. *DL* 216–22, with particular reference to painting; also *PH* 44–45; *TL* 275.

37. *RPL* 101, 103. Kristeva is restricting the word "text" to apply to a particular practice, not to any body of writing, as the word is commonly used. For "heterogeneity" and the text, see esp. *RPL* 178–81.

38. For references to Kristeva on the imagination, see above, note 10. Williams's emphasis on process is particularly strong in the discussion of the imagination in "The Basis of Faith in Art" (ca. 1937; *SE* 187–88), from which I quote below (see note 40).

39. Quoted in Sister Bernetta Quinn, "*Paterson*: Landscape and Dream," *Journal of Modern Literature* 1 (1971): 546. My transcription of the manuscript (Yale) differs from Quinn's in some accidentals.

40. *SE* 188. Moreover, the goal of redistribution argues against the finality of any specific identification of "the two sides" to which Williams refers. A draft refers to "both sides the picture" in the context of a distinction between "the poor" and "the old men" (Yale), but the reference to "two sides" in the published version seems deliberately more abstract. For more on the question of the two sides, see Terence Diggory, "The Reader in Williams and Brueghel: *Paterson* 5 and *The Adoration of the Kings*," *Criticism* 30 (1988): 366–67.

41. Lévi-Strauss, *Tristes Tropiques*, trans. John and Doreen Weightman (New York: Atheneum, 1974), 330. Walter Gibson (*Bruegel* [New York: Oxford University Press, 1977], 9) accounts for Brueghel's popularity in the twentieth century by suggesting that the artist offers an image of an Arcadian past. The role of color in evoking this image is discussed by Lawrence Gowing, "Brueghel's World," in Thomas B. Hess and John Ashbery, eds., *Narrative Art*, *Art News* Annual 36 (New York: Macmillan, 1970), 23–24, following Adrian Stokes, *Colour and Form*, 2d ed. (London: Faber, 1950), 115, 117.

 *Index*

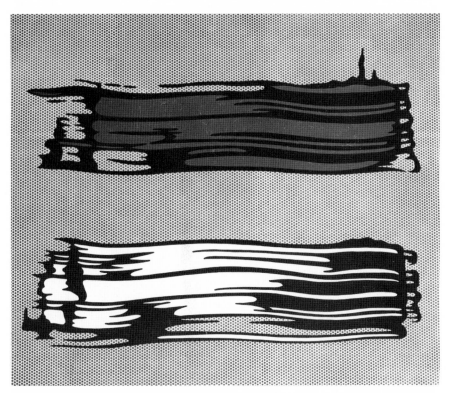

1. Roy Lichtenstein, *Yellow and Red Brushstrokes* (1966). © Roy Lichtenstein.

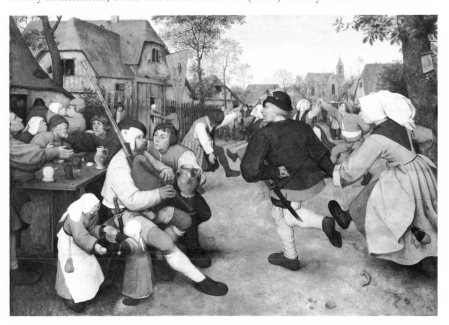

2. Peter Brueghel the Elder, *The Peasant Dance* (ca. 1567). Kunsthistorisches Museum, Vienna.

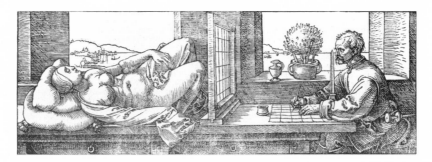

3. Albrecht Dürer, *Draftsman Drawing a Nude* (1538). The British Museum, London.

4. Jan Vermeer, *The Music Lesson* (ca. 1662). The Royal Collection, London. Copyright reserved to Her Majesty Queen Elizabeth II.

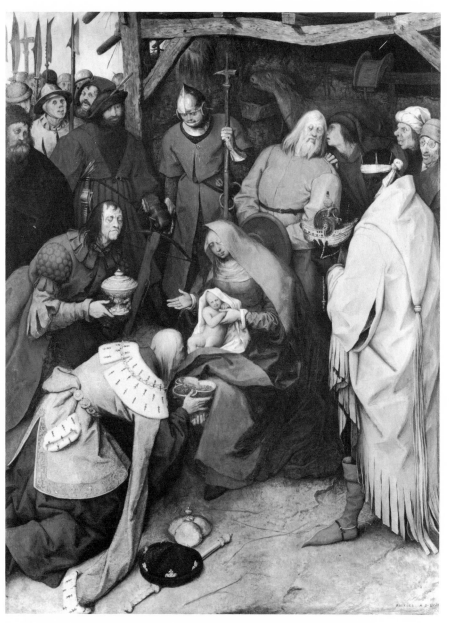

5. Peter Brueghel the Elder, *The Adoration of the Kings* (1564). The National Gallery, London.

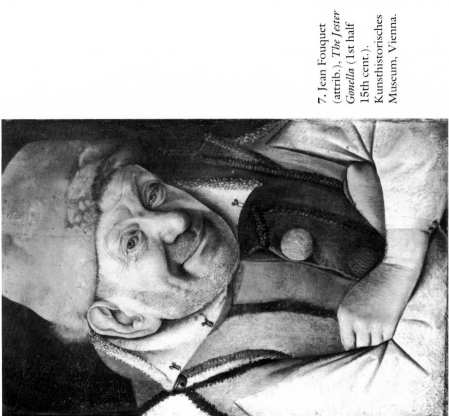

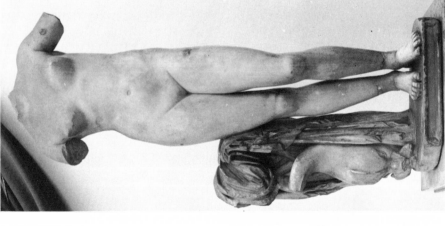

7. Jean Fouquet (attrib.), *The Jester Gonella* (1st half 15th cent.). Kunsthistorisches Museum, Vienna.

6. Aphrodite from Cyrene (2d cent. A.D. Roman copy from 4th cent. B.C. Greek original). Museo Nazionale Romano delle Terme, Rome.

8. Peter Brueghel the Elder, *The Massacre of the Innocents* (ca. 1565–1567). Kunsthistorisches Museum, Vienna.

9. Peter Brueghel the Elder, *Big Fish Eat Little Fish* (1557). The British Museum, London.

10. Fra Angelico, *Annunciation* (ca. 1440). Museo San Marco, Florence.

11. Dying lioness (Assyrian, 7th cent. B.C.). The British Museum, London.

12. Peter Brueghel the Elder, *Landscape with the Fall of Icarus* (ca. 1555). Musées Royaux des Beaux-Arts de Belgique, Brussels. Copyright A.C.L.—Brussels.

13. Hans Holbein the Younger, *Jean de Dinteville and Georges de Selve* ("*The Ambassadors*") (1533). The National Gallery, London.

14. Fragments of 5th tapestry, The Unicorn Tapestries (French or Flemish, late 15th cent.). The Metropolitan Museum of Art, New York: The Cloisters Collection.

15. Giovanni
Bellini, *Lochis Ma-
donna* (ca. 1470–
1475). Accademia
Carrara di Belle
Arti, Bergamo.

16. Romare Bear-
den, *Women with
an Oracle* (1947).

17. Albrecht Dürer, *Melancholia I*, 2d state (1514). The British Museum, London.

18. Paul Gauguin, *The Spirit of the Dead Watching* (*Manao tupapau*) (1892). Albright-Knox Art Gallery, Buffalo, New York.

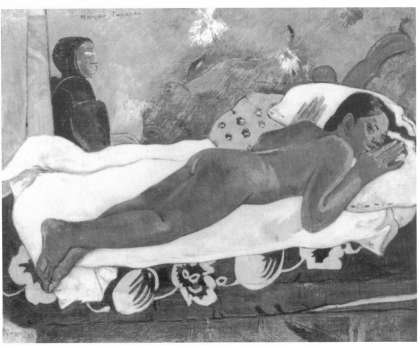

19. Paul Gauguin, *The Loss of Virginity* (1890). The Chrysler Museum, Norfolk, Virginia.

20. Henri Matisse, *Blue Nude* ("*Souvenir de Biskra*") (1907). The Baltimore Museum of Art.

21. 7th tapestry, The Unicorn Tapestries (French or Flemish, late 15th cent.). The Metropolitan Museum of Art, New York: The Cloisters Collection.

22. Juan Gris, *The Open Window* (1921). Coll. M. Meyer-Mahler, Zurich.

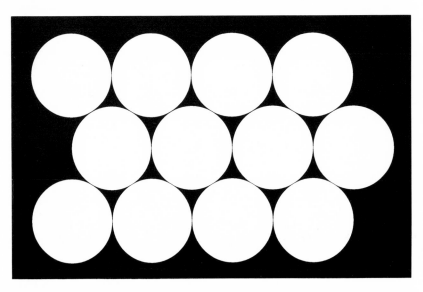

23. "White circular discs grouped closely edge to edge" (*SE* 129). (Anne P. Diggory)

24. Peter Brueghel the Elder, *The Wedding Dance* (ca. 1566). © The Detroit Institute of Arts.